A BOOK OF RANDOMNESS

DENIS SO

authorHOUSE®

AuthorHouse™
1663 Liberty Drive
Bloomington, IN 47403
www.authorhouse.com
Phone: 833-262-8899

Published by AuthorHouse 11/27/2020

ISBN: 978-1-6655-0931-2 (sc)
ISBN: 978-1-6655-0930-5 (e)

Library of Congress Control Number: 2020923634

CHAPTER 1

....

<u>A book of randomness.</u>
<u>For you, about something</u>
<u>Or nothing???</u>

A quick poem, about brain injury, 12 years on!!!

Bang!!!
Did I hear a starting gun, go off???
In mee head???

Looking back, over the years.
I had too, start from fresh again!!!
Like, walk, talk, sing and dance!!! (badly, it'll look like,
moi building a house)
Only with, my old memories.
Of not knowing, how too, sing and dance.
AND STILL DON'T!!!

BECAUSE I'm A, LAZY ASS FOOL, OVER
AND OUT!!!
Well that was, a quick intro for YOU, will the rest, make
sense too yee??? Or will I...

You've kinda reading the book, in that a paragraph,
I guess??? You can??? Toss the book, up in the air??? And
hope it lands, back down closed??? And do, whatever you've

planned for that day??? Or if you're a, curios cat??? Then you'll read on???

First off, I would like too, THANK YOU!!!

You've just done the, book title!!!

50/50, you went out, to buy this book, or came across it??? So you've helped, moi/us??? That's anyone, who has had, a brain injury, that attend, brain injury group UK, (it was the forth 1 down, on Google search in 2019, you or this book, might just bring it up???) and now the NHS, because I heard, on the news on the 17/8/15, NHS might be bankrupted, I don't want that too happen!!! Well, they did keep moi alive, so I've got to return the favour to them, and I have to help you, and now the NHS, with this book!!!! I'll still do the 50/50 part, meaning 50% in my pocket, and 50% to charity, then charity does it's own 50/50, 50 this year, then 50 for next year, but I have too explain myself, still 50/50, but the NHS, will get the first 50/50 part, then the 50 left over from the NHS, then 50/50 again, for the British Red cross, and finally Brain injury group UK, if any left??? It'll go too Oxfam, if any odd numbers??? Like £120 I'll have to round up to the nearest hundred, so it'll be £200, and then 50 50 again, that year 50 left over, goes into next years pot, so maybe an eternal funding???

Now it'll be, the NHS first, because I'm back too help everyone in the UK, then the Red cross because I have too save the world, then Brain injury group UK, WHY ARE THEY THIRD???

It goes down too my own situation, we did have a lady, working for Brain injury group UK, I did give the book too her, she told me too change something??? Did so because

I'm a bad boy??? Sent her redone version, it was with her for 3 months, maybe more??? Then her contract ended, book still not released, so she told moi, too speak to my link Brain of injury group UK or my group branch manager, how too write the next part???

And the money left??? Or my half, I've decided to help the UK.

I'll let your imagination wondering??? Or you can, pop over too, Salisbury to meet her??? Or meet us in SMP, Salisbury Medical Paratactic, on Thursday from 10:00 am – 13:30 pm, the year 2019 onwards??? Say your here, because my book told you to pop on down, and if you want a squiggle in your book, too prove we've met me in person??? I'll have to date it, so on that day, we met.

Don't forget your **** and shield, NAH just messing with your mind, because I'm driving your mind, ah left turn!!!

I heard on the news, on the 21/9/15, that England, will have a lot of, Dementia cases, can I bring, the cure to dementia, to England??? I said, how to later on, in mee book, I think the news, got dementia, mixed up with Alzheimer's, to my understanding is, Alzheimer's is forgetting how to do things, and Dementia is, forgetting thing that just happened to you, 30 Min's ago, if it's bad??? But worse or/advanced, if only 20 Min's, but Alzheimer's is part of Dementia, but they are 2 different types of illness, in one, but the same, illness at the end of the day, not being able to create new brain cells, that is the sickness!!!

They say, "you are never, too old, too learn!!!" But it's a catch 22, you can, only learn the small things in life, or add, more to your current knowledge??? You can't, replace your mother tongue, just add another language on top!!! Will some1 prove moi wrong???

You can't replace, your mother tongue??? I think???

Because that's the, first language you learn, it'll stays with you, until the day you die???

But if you suffer, or have dementia, then your brain is, too old to learn!!! Meaning, you have over worked your brain, or it's hereditary, or in mee case, accident meaning, no more, new brain cells, created for you!!!

That's why, the brain looks like, it is, due to using speech everyday, and movement, as well.

I'm a, theory FOOL!!! That's why, I call this book 50/50, I'm just giving you, a heads up, on the afterlife, and from my experience of death, if doing this 50/50, that will affect your, afterlife???

SORRY my poor use of maths!!!

50/50 would work, if I, didn't take a cut of the money!!! So it's more like, 12.5 % back too moi!!! So that's, 25 % too Brain of injury group UK, 25 % too the NHS, 25 % too who ever is the company??? That releases this book??? And 12.5 % to moi, 5 % too Oxfam, because in 2014, they kinda rob my broken ass, because I went away, for medical treatment, and they didn't give moi, an end of year meal, for my hard work that year!!! But PLEASE, STILL GO TOO THERE SHOP!!! AND SUPPORT THEM!!! It's just a, thing that has happened to moi!!! The British red cross 7.5 %, because I'm still working for them!!!

CHAPTER 2

....

Start off, I use to be an, office boy, or an admin assistant, I just turned 25, they say, it takes that long, for the brain to mature, then I had too, start life again, at 25 years old, my accident was a late gift or birthday present, I mean 6 days after my birthday, and the gift, was starting life again!!! Not even a week, for it to be, just a miss hap!!! And the bonus, is the left side of my brain, got wasted!!! Or damaged, we know, the opposite side of are brain, controls are body, like I use to be right handed, meaning the left side, of my brain, was more dominate, but not right handed anymore, then moved on to being left handed, but now, a freak!!! Ambidextrous freak!!! If you, don't know that word??? It means, being able to use, both hands, for everything.

Well not quite, only simple things, like simple writing, not an advanced ambidextrous person, I can only use chopsticks, well in my left hand, but seem to go back, to my, old skool style of holding chopsticks in, my right hand, just not well!!!

What happened to moi(me), I was driving, but nature, decided to make the roads have black ice, the police say, as I was young, so I must of been speeding(25 YEARS OLD)!!!

But I have my, own rule, don't break the law, in your own town, you live in!!!

Meaning, I use too, stick to the speed limit, in my own town!!!

But speed in other towns!!!

And do close call driving, or over taking, if I crashed??? Then that's a, major lose, too moi(me).

I've only broke the law once!!!

It was 3 am, in the morning, when I engaged, Vtec in my Honda civic, 1.8 vti, it was the first week, I had owned the car, you know what they say??? New toy, got to be played with, or tested out???

It was down, Brown street, it's the longest straight road, in Salisbury town centre, I hit 60+ mph, and still had, more gears to go, I only used 2 gears.

It was after my test, I decided, not to engage Vtec!!!

In my own town!!!

&I use to be a taxi driver, for my friend, we call him Oak, but his full name is Mark Oakley, his friends, called him Oak, we just shorten his Surname down from, Oakley to Oak, all the times I was his taxi driver, from the train station in town, to his mums house, in Harnham, I never engaged Vtec, and it was, a 2 mile drive/journey to his mums house in Harnham, every Thursday night, back in 2003-don't remember when I stopped??? Maybe??? When I had my, VIP trip???

If I repeat myself???

You are not, crazy!!!

It's just my mind, has slipped, once or maybe twice, and maybe again??? The third time LUCKY???

Life is???

My version is, all about the food!!!

We can get our, grubs on too eat!!!

(I should say "hands" to be, PC or politically correct, ah well, never mind!!!)

We live in, the catch 22 reality, doing one thing, benefits another thing down the line, but we need patience with time!!!

Like when you, have a shower, in the summer time, do you use warm water to clean your body, but that, has opened up all your pours, which will lead, you to sweating again, after your shower, but you need a cold rinse, to close up, all your pours, to stay dry from sweating again!!! I know that sounds like, PURE INSANITY!!! Just bite the bullet, and do it!!!

Like when you drive your car, do you warm up, the engine, before you drive it???

Because technology, has made us all, lazier, to go to places, to get our stuff done!!! But science stays the same!!! Meaning we need the time to heat up liquids in the engine, and that takes time, your time, well I have an idea???

This thinking, goes back, to the carburettor, days in car engines, I had to warm up, my Pug(Peugeot) 205 Rallye, to run well, and not stall, then that thinking, goes out the window, when I had a fuel injected car, I also use to warm up, the carburettor engine, when I/we, me and my brother, left our friend house, Oak, late at night.

But I didn't know then, you use more fuel, to move the engine parts in the morning!!! To get where you are going, and that'll increase your mpg reading, we all have been, brain washed, by F1, filling up, are fuel tank, to the top, but that is with a warm engine, and it only weighing, 702 kg, including the driver. If you, have a 50+ mile journey next, it'll be alright, not so, if your going home, to sleep!!! That is, the best way, too warm up, a performance engine!!! But it's not the same, with a family run about car, which you use everyday!!!

Meaning more trips to the pumps = less money, in your pocket!!!

It also has, a domino effect, on filling up your car fuel tank, I mean, you'll do it more often, as you have increased the mpg rating, are you, that wealthy, enough to do that??? And do you get a pay rise every week??? To cover your increased mpg rating every week??? And not to mention, that you will, push up, the price of fuel, again!!!

If your car??? Is fuel injected??? A ¼ warm, saves you about 20 miles, if fully warmed up??? You can get back 38 miles back, but that information, is from, the 1st generation, of fuel injected cars, how far is that too you now???

I've come up with an idea??? (ONLY IN THE, PERFECT WORLD, WHERE CARS ARE NOT, STOLEN!!!)

If you have time to kill???

It's to start up the car up, if fuel injected, do you, just go, and use more fuel???

Or do you sit there, warming up the car engine???

It takes about 30 minutes with the fan turned too, off/cold, for the needle, on the temp gauge, to reach the middle, as you won't be stealing the heat, from the engine, to warm up the cabin, if engine warmed up??? You'll have a warmer cabin/car to drive to work in or to have a warm engine, science says, you can and should, get up 30 minutes, before your normal, wake up time, if done???

Then you'll have, your 30 minutes, of car warming up time then!!!

And it'll save you money, in the long run, because you,

don't have to buy de-icer, for your car, because it'll be warm enough, to melt the ice on the car, if it's winter time???

See I've given you, another 50/50, choice in life again.

I sort of, have an idea for you too try out??? (only in the perfect world, where cars are not stolen!!!)

Start the car up, turn the heating off in the car, or too cold, and also, put your heated rear wind screen on, if winter time, to melt the ice on the rear wind screen, then your heating system won't be, stealing the heating, from the engine!!! When the rear window, has melted, put the heating on in the car to full blast, to have a warm car, Then go back in the house, go put the kettle on, when boiled, have a tea/coffee, or a cofftea??? Drink that down, when done, the engine may have warmed up??? And the car too, then you'll be driving a toastie car, to work in, if winter time???

But technology, has moved on sooo much now, it'll take, a minute – 3 minutes, too warm up your car now??? That is, kinda BS, to moi!!! it's more like, 12 minutes just to get, the temperature needle off the cold mark on the temp gauge, still 30 minutes, to be warm!!!

The devil, plays the cold engine and extra weight, you have to move around in your car!!!

Like the average reading, for the cars mpg, that is done!!!

On an engine dyno, with just the engine, no body shell, and no people!!! In the car!!!

I think they should do it, with the shell, and throw in 100 KG, as 1 person, driving the car!!!

I know, that's 1, fat person (100KG, I'm only 73 KG, or am I???)

Now the average, family car, is about a tonne, on it's own, no people in there, so when you add the people in there, it'll not be the average mpg, due to the extra weight, and the test is done, on an engine dyno machine, or just the engine on the dyno machine!!! The car engine is, out of the car, meaning it'll run off, too no where, then they have a reading, when it's out of fuel, it's only just the weight of the engine, on it's own.

This information is for Brain of injury group UK, a national charity, I'm in a branch/link of it, or the South Coast branch now, and use to, go down to Southampton or Totton Brain of injury group UK, every Tuesday, as well, but they capped my, Asian black ass & raped, me too, or to be PC(Politicly Correct) about it, they banned my ass, for not reading, my whole message, too them!!!

An old Asian, saying goes, but now the Americans, have taken it over!!! It goes, "you have to read, the full story!!! Too, understand it, or the ending of it, to know, the outcome!!! Don't do the mother of all f-ups, an assumption!!! On my Asian black ass, or my broken black ass now!!! If you use any of my, randomness to pass on to other people??? You'll be cheating on charity!!! I kinda, live the old skool way, in life, they don't, as they are unbroken, or they just do, the worse outcome in life, or an assumption on your broken ass!!!

Well I think???

All physiologist, no matter, what ever category, they specialize in, should read, the whole story!!!

Because, all the words came from, one mind!!!

You probably won't, go to Totton Brain of injury group UK, and ask for, my printed out wrongness, to read it???

You probably won't, get the follow up messages, after my first, mind rape, it should have been, "I'll love rape you", if you remember, back to 1995, when everyone, was spreading the love!!!

It was an, American saying, we just added a word, same thing, but we just didn't say, spreading the "love", just threw are arms around them, then when releasing them, we just said, "you've just been love raped!!!"

Meaning, there is, physical proof, out there of my, wrongness!!!

Another way, I look at life is??? Life is a journey, with challenges, thrown in, to make it, more interesting, pour (for) him to watch us, perform for him!!!

We all go to, the same place, at the end of the day!!!

Born when your, journey starts, learn how to walk and talk, sing and dance, if that's your thing??? Then education kicks in!!!

Do you live and learn, aiming to reach something, I don't know what???

It's your life!!!

Can you choose, please???

That's why, life is a journey!!!

You live, so you must, have to die!!!

And it's also, one big circle, for life itself!!! born learn, work, maybe reproduce??? Then die, become worm food??? Well not quite a circle, more like a straight line for us!!!

Because you, won't be, born again!!!

If a large person dies???

Party time for the worms, if they get too eat your body???

As they say "spread the love!!!"

And that's what you are doing!!!

Feeding the worms your body, will you be worm food??? Or will you not???

CHAPTER 3

Will this be a story, a novel, or will it be, about, fact/fiction, to you???

Well it's fact to me!!! Because, it happened to me, it'll be a heads ups for you, when your time is up down here!!!

Another thing is, being ill with a brain injury, it, kinda takes the piss!!!

If you do get ill???

I sort of had, a good immune system, or did have???

It takes, a long time too get well again!!!

Well, I'm all good, a few days into being ill, but my busted brain, says "hold on, my black Asian fool!!!"

A wee bit left, to fight off, to go back to, being black again!!!

Why do I calls this story 50/50???

It's Win/lose???

That also goes for, my mind, logical or non logical = stupidness???

You can either donate to charity???

Or walk on in your life???

50/50 for you???

I'm going to, try to explain, a brain injury, it's like a never ending story!!! Not the film.

You just have too, keep on pushing yourself!!!

There is NO!!! Time frame, for a brain injury, to be put

in, like broken limbs, e.g. arms, or legs, just keep on going, well the other side of the coin is, DEATH!!!

But I've been put back to be, challenged!!! Or to be evil???

I read this information somewhere, they also included picture's or images, so I'm, kinda, relying on your imagination here??? Well I'm kinda of borrowing there information, but not using, there pictures or images!!! Just your, imagination, think of your body, as a battery or battery cell, when you wake up, everyday or morning, your body and brain are, fully charged, then reduces, over the 24 hour cycle, wake up and eat food, aka breakfast, because you have a 35-40 minute, dead line time, then go brush your teeth, or brush your teeth first, then eat, why that way round??? It's because, your saliva, is in food burning mode, and it'll burn away the eminimal found on your teeth!!! and then get changed, I think you've used up 1%, of your energy, then do the same old, same old, that's go to work, then you've used about 10% of energy, by 10 am??? take another, 10% off it, by the time it gets to midday, then carry on, by the time, you call it a days work, your down to 48%, then do your evening or night time actives, then at 9pm, you have 28% left, then time for bed, too recharge your battery cell (aka body).

Now with a brain injury, you wake up, 99% full, do your stuff, by 10 am, you can take off 30%, if you go to work??? When done, your left with 12% of energy, and it's ONLY 6 PM!!!

Then do your evening actives, then it's empty at 8pm, then time to recharge your body and brain.

(this is, only a guesstimation for tu, as everyone is different???)

That's why, we need to sleep/rest a lot, it's to fix our broken brain, we need to fix our brain a lot after an accident/sickness???

Life is an unwritten script, or journey, the end is when your life is up/over/become worm food??? Or when your done down here!!!

Life is made up of choices you make???

CHAPTER 4

....

But I've been a fool, with my choice, Because I remember, listening too, 2 people, who are older, then me, as they say, "respect your elders!!!" well come to think about it??? They thought, that being a mechanic, was all the same, but not for, the company I was working for, it was, to train, to the company's standards, or no job!!! But no names, said to you, more likely fiction, because I've had a brain injury, you'll say!!! It's just my written down, random memories, for you.

My thinking, maybe wrong, and a little bit random!!!

Like life, has bitched slapped moi, really dam good!!!

There is also, a saying, "quick gain, long term pain" I modified my car, quick gain, followed with, as I write this story, it's been 12 years with no driving, my long term, pain!!!

Well that's just moi(me), see I was, random, in writing, French to you!!!

Cos life is a gamble, you can either win/lose???

Or live/die???

50/50???

But that's just moi (me)!!!

That's why I'm back, to gamble, and to be random, and make you gamble, as well if you read this book/story???

I haven't, gambled, with my life, until, the 13/10/13 when I did a 3 mile walk, with no walking stick, too rely on!!!

The night before the walk day, Sarah Allen, text me to

say, "I think? You should bring, your stick!!! The ground, maybe uneven!!!"

That's logic speaking for you!!!

Now I'm an illogical fool/gambler, logic = being safe to me, I wonder why??? Do you want to be safe??? Is it too grow old, and pee in your own pants again, or just DIE, trying???

But I am a, hardcore gambler!!! Aka stubborn mofo, or in Cantonese, they say, hard neck.

I did the walk, with no trips/falls, and it has been, 6 years+, using a stick to help moi(me)walk.

If I/you die???

Fate wants you gone/the dude thinks, you are, way too boring, for him, to watch you???

If this gets, put on TV??? Or made into a movie???

I don't think??? You can, find anyone, as fat as moi(me)???

I'll say to you, can you please, donate 3 million, in what ever currency you'll be showing it in or at???

As the saying goes best of 3, or out of 3, mmm if I was asking for more then it'll be 33 million, or super greedy, 333 million or if extra super greedy, 3 billion.

Sorry to say, you'll be cheating, on the charity, I'm in now!!! By passing on information, that I've come back with!!!

Or I can remember???

I can remember, meeting the dude (GOD/lord), in his TV room, I don't know why, my memory is so detailed, in remembering random stuff??? It's the, white light people, say they can see/remember, when they come back to Earth!!! It's because of the TV's, in his room, that give off the white light, that people say they have seen, when they have died, and have come back down to Earth!!! Another film link is,

"The Matrix", so we have had a glimpse, into GODS life already.

Well, that's what I think is, the white light???

It is his TV, and it's dam good!!!

He also likes to play, the card of irony, on your ass!!!

Because, he knew, I don't speed, in my own town, and he also knew, I had learnt, how to control, a car sliding, but that's only in, a rwd car, rear wheel drive car not a fwd car, front wheel drive car, which are mainly, Honda cars, that's why black ice for me!!!

I was in a coma for 3 months, I went to his TV room & he's munching on a bucket of fried sprit chicken, when he's watching us perform for him, even thou he is a spirit, a guesstimate for you???

That's a word, I made up, it's guess and estimate, they kinda, mean the same thing, I just put them together to make one word = guesstimate.

It's so boring, only using one word, like I guess, or estimate, it's just not interesting, to moi.

With over 63 billion channels to choose from!!! My broken memory, goes back too, when I was still in secondary school back in 1998, the world population was, only 52 billion!!! My thinking goes??? We thought, we need to be, married, to have children!!! That's why 63 billion in 2016, It's us, we are on his TV, his mind is linked to all of us, through telepathy, and he knew, I had a good memory, before my crash, because, it goes back, to the 27/8/86, I was only 3 years old & a 1/2 when I went, with my dad, to go see, a shop space, before it was, turned into the, Chef Peking, it's dam good, because the script is unwritten, so it's never a re-run, of the same show, if you win a competition, he wants you to perform for him, and give him a free plug.

E.g. Kelly Clarkson.

We are all are, unpaid actors for him, that is are payment, for us when we die!!! Do we go to heaven/hell???

Your life story, will decide, for you???

Well we've all got a green book, or you know it as, your life story, all the thing you say and do, gets written in it, by fairies, even thou, you can't remember saying it, cos it'll come back round and kick you in the ass, when your dead, or have died/when your done down here??? Because you put your book through a computer to read, when you die, it'll read everything, you've done while your down here on earth!!! And it will say, heaven/hell for you???

I spent a month in Southampton's ICU, then moved to Salisbury Odstock hospital, was there for 3 or 4 weeks, then moved to Bath for 8 months, then on to Glenside for 7 months, and now back home.

CHAPTER 5

....

Constantine the movie is correct!!!

The dude, and the devil, are twins, 1 good and 1 evil, that's where the saying, comes from, 1 good and 1 evil, 50/50 for you, they made a deal, on all of are souls, but absolutely, no contact!!! With us, that's why I call this the 50/50 reality, good/bad you choose???

Just only things, to make you/us decide, if we take the good route/bad route in life???

Some of the information, I'll be talking about, my seem religious to you, but it isn't, because I've, met the man/dude, aka GOD, but I call HIM, the dude & he's my niggar now, it's because, he sent me back, to eat chicken, because, he loves it too!!!

Well after my head injury, all my symptoms, may look physical.

But it's not!!!

I think TBI (Traumatic, Brain, Injury) can be put into 2 groups/categories???

1, is just the skull being opened, in a controlled environment/situations, like surgery, you still got your sleeping brain intact, I guesstimate???

2, is a deep injury, meaning you've got to start, life again, but still got all your old memories, but don't, even know, when you are, asleep. (like moi(me), I really don't know why, my mind is writing simple, François or French in English???)

Because my brain got injured, the main control unit for your body!!!

CHAPTER 6

It's why people, who just have a broken limb, can heal from it, because there brain makes, new brain cells/a new path way in there brain, due to being able to create new brain cells, anyone who has had a brain injury can't!!! That's the other thing about the whole brain, it can create new brain cells, as we know the brain is divided up into different sections, but there is no section to create new brain cells!!! It's because the whole brain is 1 big mussel, being able to create new brain cells in that section/area, or all over it???

It's why I have been removed from the group of norm!!!

Well I'm half a zombie, cos I'm a walking dead person, I remember being dead & going to the waiting room, I call it, it's the room where, the dude, decides if you live/die??? And you get to see, how your life, could of turned out??? If you took, a different path in your life or not, in your life???

Because he has done his own version of are lives, down here??? Which means, I'm a dead boring LOGICAL FOOL, in the other reality, but I hear you say, "it's ALL GOOD!!! BEING SAFE AND BORING!!! That's WHY, I like to walk, on the wild side of life. it's just PURELY RANDOM, for him to watch moi then, who knows??? Will I live or die???

In the other reality, that has happened, someone had asked moi, or I asked someone something??? I remember meeting the dude AKA GOD. But he took the image of his face, from my memory, because he can, as he made us, so it's just an outline of him!!! Or a shaded shadow of a shape of a man.

Because I've lost the ability, to create new brain cells, that's why, old people have white hairs and there age comes into it as well, it's because they have lots of brain cells, I started to have white hairs, when I was only 14 years old, and had more, then my cousin, in Hk (Hong Kong) and he's two years older then me!!! It was due to me being a film buff, back in secondary school, I watched a new film every week, with friends, back in secondary school, but now I've been returned to the age of 0 again mentally, so no white hairs now, but getting them again, because I'm an oldie, and I'm 11 years old now, well mentally now, old people can remember along time ago, that's why they have white hairs, and there age comes into play, cos when your older you lose colour pigments in your hair, that's why when your old, you get white hairs, I can't take down any new information spoken to me, now!!! Due to me losing, the ability to create new brain cells!!!

It's also known as "Dementia", if you've had a brain injury???

You have been advance to being an oldie!!!

Because my mum is 60 years old in 2012, it's due to having stale blood in your head, so when your young go exercise to move the blood around your body, The age limit is 30 years old??? Or maybe 40??? I guesstimate??? Nah, my mum seems, too be getting better now, going to the gym with me, moving her blood round, in her body&brain.

Like when we, go to the gym, there is just is a random girl on the reception, my mum remembers, 2 nice girls, but different girls, 1 is British blond girl who is called Vicky, who is nice to us, 2 is an American girl, who just started she is called Michelle with brown or brunette hair.

But I think my mum, still has the ability, but only the things she wants to remember.

Well I sort of, got that ability back, with Acupuncture, the medical thing he left for us to use!!! And it was used in the movie, "The Matrix" It's an Eastern and Western mix movie, it's what it'll be like when dead!!!

Can England, allow the use for longer needles in Acupuncture??? Because my doctor in Hk, said England uses shorter needles, he would rather heal his customers, once, so they only pay him once.

Another way, I think is going back to, when you're learning, to remember stuff, as a child, matching up card pairs, I think that's a way to create new brain cells???

I've worked out what alcohol is???

It's the devil's blood!!! It because they need to escape this reality, or the situation they are in/you are in, by drinking his blood.

Because he is a spirit now, as he can't, come into this physical realm???

So why not give us alcohol, because you get a moment of pleasure, then gets killing right away, when you drink it, your brain cells, gets killed right away!!!

That's why your pee pee, is so dark yellow, it's your dead, brain cells, leaving your body.

Why do we have money???

Well both of them decided, we need something to be able to divide us up, and it's money!!!

Then the devil decided to make it/them, his children, which is evil!!!

Wanting his children, aka imps, that's how they came too be, or are formed, and he'll be, your new dead buddy, playing with your soul, until I don't know when, he'll stop???

As it's a soulless object, and wanting, a soulless object is evil!!! So you're wanting nothing!!!

So, you want to be friends, with the devil then???

Wanting and needing his children???

My style of exercise I call it 50/50, because you have to go that far, to do it, it's weather you live/die, 50/50, for you, you have to go pass tiredness and keep pushing on, who knows the out come???

That's why it's 50/50, who knows what will happen too you??? The 50/50 part, and gives your body a warmer core/higher internal core temperature, I believe you are, pushing out the warmness of your body, just my theory on that situation??? if you have, normal blood circulation, then you'll have sweaty hands, due to a better blood circulation in your body, being dam good!!! & hot too.

But now I'm just a warm fool, due to my blood circulation, slowing down, after my car crash, that is 1 of the unseen symptom, and sometimes, I feel cold, but still have a warm body, that's down to poor blood circulation.

I think, I sort of know, why people wear glasses??? Well it is a memory from infant school.

It's their brain holding on, too much information in it, then your brain decides to reduce your visual need for the space, that's why you need to wear glasses.

I can sort of do an example???

I need glasses due to me getting a distinction, and merit, in T+T, Travel and Tourism, and a friend called Sidney Soh, he got a distinction in business studies, we both wear glasses, but he has had an operation, his brother doesn't wear glasses, he done product design, and he did choose to do that subject as well, but only got a merit, I know you'll say it is harder!!! But he did choose to go study it, so why didn't, he get a distinction??? Another theory, I have is, they are the first child in the family, and the same goes for my eldest sister, they only believe in written down facts!!! And there mind isn't random enough, for them to wear glasses. The three younger siblings in my family, do wear glasses, and they say it's a DNA thing, and my dad, wears glasses, so why not her??? Like I said, the three younger siblings do??? And another thing comes to mind is, spoken language, is either small space, used up in our brain, or not enough room to need glasses??? And again, my 2 examples are the 2, eldest children again, but Sidney brother, knows 3 languages, sort of well, my eldest sister knows 2 languages, well, not as I don't want to say it, because if I do, I'll sound like if I've got a Hugh head/big headed!!!

why do people drink, alcohol and smoke???

CHAPTER 7

Alcohol can lead to early Dementia, it's because it destroys, new brain cells, or stops you from creating new ones, cos your brain is drenched in alcohol!!! My mum said in HK (Hong Kong), they done the research into alcohol, and it does cause Dementia, early it was back in 2013, they did the research.

When the dude, came down with me, he told me why!!!

It's due to them having a small brain, and it got me thinking???

When the chemical goes into there body, there brain says to them, this is dam good shit, my niggar!!!

Do more!!! Mee niggar!!!

If you have a big brain, the chemical can't please your brain, and it taste like petrol??? And only make you sick if it's alcohol, due to your body trying to get rid of the liquid that you have just drank, you only just cough, due to smoking, it's due to the smoke filling up your lungs, and not pleasing your brain.

I can't believe, when I was 5, I took a swig of beer, in are restaurant, then called "Chef Peking" and nothing happen to me!!! & when I was, 8 years old, I asked a former chef in are restaurant, why do you smoke???

He couldn't explain it, and just gave me a cigarette to smoke, he lit it up in my mouth, and I took 1 drag or inhale of it, nothing but when the smoke filled up my lungs, I coughed the smoke back out.

It's due to my body getting rid of the smoke in my lungs, I said why you get sick, when having alcohol, it's the same with smoking, it's just, the chemical not pleasing your brain, and your body, wants to get rid of it!!!

&he told me, it's the man to decided, if you have any children or not, it was in the movie, X men, it's the man, who has the mutant X gene, and this world is full of selfish fools, because I believe??? 75% of the world is full of girls, I guesstimate???

If it were boys, then he wants your attitude to live on!!! As there is, a saying "you can, teach your child, everything in life, but they will only learn, your attitude, at the end of the day!!!"

I would put in an example for you, but don't have permission, to tell you, in written language form, for you. :(D.

I'll be talking about a list given to me by a psychologist on how to reduction emotional vulnerability.

1, is treat physical illness.

2, is balance eating.

3, is avoid mood-altering drugs / alcohol.

4, is balance sleeping.

5, is get exercise.

6, is build mastery or gain a sense of achievement.

My random take on is:

1, is treat physical illness, well I thought, I'll do a 50/50 thing with it, cause pain for your body to fix the injury faster, how, wrong was I??? I needed lots of rest to fix my ankle/leg, holding too much omega 3 in it, from the pills

I've been taking, as I'm a broken fool, my body can't reduce the omega 3 oil, I've taken in, and disperse it in one day!!!

2, is balance eating, well fatness does not help you, it gives you more of a challenge, to move you around!!! And you!!!

Please don't, eat apple seeds, because your mind, will go, to the negative side in your life!!!

Someone told moi, they are, poisonous!!!

Well my mind went, they are so small, how could, they poison moi???

Well as my brain, is broken, it made my thinking, so negative, to me!!!

3, is avoid mood-altering drugs/alcohol, that's asking the devil to help you out, to over come your problem, but will, kick you, in the nuts, when it's gone!!!

4, is balance sleeping, if you've had a brain injury, your sleeping pattern goes out the window, it's 1 of the things, that being able to create new brain cells, I believe??? It'll help you to sleep well at night, because sleep is for your brain to fix itself, and if you had a brain injury, your brain needs fixing, more often then others.

&your brain is saying, I need to be fixed, so sleep, my niggar!!!

There is another catch 22, having power naps, only do, 15-30 minutes Max, so I'll say go for a 25 minute kip, to start things off, there is a catch 22, you can take, 15 minutes off, your normal sleeping time, if you had 30 minutes??? Or half of the sleep time you had???

Please can you, only do 3 or 2 naps??? Nah I say 2 now!!! Because 3 naps may lead you too, 4 hour end of day sleeps, so kip for 30 minutes, twice!!! If more then 3, it'll be 45 minutes off, your normal sleep, if 3 times??? If done anymore??? You've entered the, 1 hour off, your normal sleep time!!! That means, 1 or 2 hours of sleep that day well night!!!

If you have, an over active, mind when your awake??? You'll mostly likely, have 5 hours of sleep??? Because, your mind can, repair it self quicker!!!

5-8 hour is normal, for everyone, but if your mind, is over active mind, 4-6 hours of sleep, every night, if you have a big brain??? Because your mind, can fix itself quicker!!!

The only, other person is, Sherlock Homes, I know, he is a made up charterer, but he see everything, that's happening around him.

The other living person, I was told, was Marge Thatcher.

And I kinda, found out, eating a banana, before sleep, can help you sleep for longer, it's something too do with the chemical found in them, well the first one, I tried, I sleeped for 7 HOURS!!!

But eat the banana, about 30-45 min's before you sleep, then it gives you, a bit of time too, digest it, so the chemical still in your body, because it takes about an hour, too digest fruit or an apple, well they say.

Or another way, is to do, 20 minutes of sleep or less??? Like I said, 15 minutes, is the starting point, for a power nap, That's a quick way to fix the brain/recharge it.

Hey it's your life, you can choose please???

I personally do, 19 minutes and 48 seconds, I got 7 hours of sleep that time, alright it was, 7 hours and 20 minutes of sleep, I fell, a sleep at, 22:28 pm, then woke up at 5:48 am, and I had a dream too boot as well!!!

There is another catch 22 with, the kip times, they all

add up, no matter, if it was short and sweet, or the full hog, please can you, stick too 3 kips, please, because, that'll be 45 mins, off your long sleep time!!!

I kinda found away, too get more deep sleep, it's before you, go to sleep, they say 5 minutes before, it is to, set your mind, to a positive state, so your mind is, more relaxed for sleeping, I had to do it 3 times before it worked for moi, and my results were, 5 hours 28 minutes of sleep, 3 hours 28 minutes of deep sleep, how sweet is that???

5, is get exercise, it's getting oxygen to your mussels, and it moves your blood around your body as well.

6, is build mastery or gain a sense of achievement, it makes you feel good!!! Then you can say, "in your mind??? Or to someone, in your face, ma niggar/non believer???

"Ha ha ha"

Another thing I've noticed is, sleeping over 30 mins, you may have full blown insomnia, if you own/have a large brain??? It's down too, I can see people that have a small brain, can kip for as long as they want too??? Big brain people, ah too much kip time, no kip for you later tonight then!!!

O no, now I've given a test, to all my readers, too see if they own, a small brain/large brain???

I've just given you the end result??? If done??? It's your life you can, try it out/let that shit slide???

I have quite a few personality's, I'll try to list them for you.

1, is OCD Den, who seem to be driving now.

2, is 50/50 Den, he also a gambler!!!

Because Doyal Brunson, the famous Texas hold-em

poker player, said "anyone who gambles with no money, is a hardcore gambler" e.g. life!!!

I didn't know??? It was, a sickness, called "ADHD" It's called, Attention, Deficit, Hyperactive, Disorder, the symptoms are:

- little or no sense, of danger, (that's a gamble to me!!!)
- Taking risks in actives, often with little or no regard for personal safety or the safety of others, for example, driving dangerously. (not, in the, town, I live in!!!)
- forgetfulness. (well, still, sort of, even tho, I've been half healed)
- Poor organisational skills (how with my OCD???)
- restlessness and eagerness.
- constantly fidgeting. (Well, I seem too, just let things slide).
- acting without thinking (but my mind is, always on???)

Well I just gambled on fate, do I live/die???

It's how I use to drive, but not, in the town, I live in!!!

That's why, I use to look after my car, that means, I can push my car, to the limit, and if I crashed it, it's all my fault!!! No one can take the blame!!! I have to take the blame, because my car was in top condition, and if I lived, knowing I killed someone, that's a major lose.

Everyone thinks that's crazy, but my version is, way beyond that!!!

3, Evil Den, he is a hidden evil, because he can see the evil happening around him, but doesn't say a word, it's due to the devil having, no one, too play with!!! And I'm sending people down to him, is it a good/evil thing??? It's because since the 1940's, something came into play, cos heaven is full of people that shouldn't be there!!! But I'm dived??? On the Old Sarum airfield now??? Nah I'll respect the dead!!! As there is, NO WAR GOING ON NOW??? (and I get too eat, FRIED CHICKEN NOW/WHEN I CAN, GET MEE HANDS ON SOME???)

4, Zombie Den, he was born on the 18th of December 2007, he just there in the back ground, he wants to meet some people to eat!!! E.g. look up/back a few pages??? He can't take any lives, because it's too hard to crack open the skull, and he'll be taking their life too!!!

5, Random D, he came out with 50/50 Den, when I was only 14 years old, then I got my driving licence at 18 years old, and moved my 50/50 style of living, to my car. (out of my town!!!)

6, Watching D, he just watches, the dude told me I'm doing his job down here!!!

It's what he is doing now, just watching us, perform for him, or be a fool, for him/not???

7, Cheap O Den, it's because, I know something, that involves money, that came into play in the 1940's and I just don't like to spend it!!!

Well that's all I can see for now.

I'll give you a choice, in eating food when it comes out, or wait for everyone to join you, or just wait for the chef???

Do you want to be a, fool like me???

And just wait??? Because, there is lots of room, to be a fool???

As my brother says, Japanese people, test the food for poison in it, but that was in the old days, in ancient Japan.

That's why, they eat first.

And another thing is, your teeth, can't take the heat!!! Of the cooked food, just brought out to you!!!

O yeah I've got a greed, not for money, but for flavours, I like the feeling of taste in your mouth of randomness to go off, in my mouth, I feel sorry, for the people who have lost the ability to taste, that's what it'll be like, when you are dead, cos you don't need food to live, cos your dead or a spirit.

That's why I like to eat, a bacon, tea roll, it's 2 flavours in one bite, salty and sweet.

& why not, mint sauce, with Chinese meat dumplings, it's too replace the vinegar used, that's life, too moi(me), trying out, all different kinds of foods, like I said "no need for food, when dead!!!"

Mmm randomness for you!!!

People with Anosmia, can be healed, in England, with acupuncture, it's because my doctor in Hk, said it can be cured in England.

Due to the use, of shorter needles, used for acupuncture, in England.

If my randomness, gets published in other languages???

That would be, awesome for Brain of injury group UK, for getting foreign money, into there account!!!

How far, will my randomness go???

Who knows???

Only the dude, will knows, my out come???

CHAPTER 8

··

If you speak English???

It's the language of the dudes, it's because Buddha speaks, it too, I thought??? He'll speak Cantonese to me, but no, he spoke English to me!!! It was kinda, wearied, the white dude, spoke to me, I think he was bored or something??? And I don't know, why and where Buddha came from???

I thought, he'll be looking after Asia, or watching it???

Cos they are all related, that's why we can mix are races, down here.

But there is no African DUDE, the whiteie made a mistake, with them, that's why they are good at sport/music???

He's saying "sorry, your that colour, be awesome at something, that you do!!!"

E.g. music, sport, and racing, or motor sport, I don't know, if Lewis Hamilton, will win, more F 1 titles, then Michael Schumacher, 7 titles for him to beat???

Having an open mind, is believing, in other realities, or trying out other brands??? Cos they are, or play the main part of the question???

Well no 1, has an open mind, cos everyone is in there own world, if everyone, believed in the same thing, this reality, would be sooo boring, to watch for him/them!!!

I have been removed, from that group, it's because I've met the whiteie, and have 2 scares on my body, when I was hooked up to life support machines, to prove I did go from down here!!!

It's kinda awesome, I've 2 belly buttons now, 1 is your normal 1, the other 1, was for my feeding tube, to keep moi alive.

My random mind came up with this, the universe is the dad, of the dudes, the universe made everything, and put the dudes into entertain him, then the dude, made dinosaurs, but all they did do, was, sleep, shit and just eat, then made us, to entertain him.

So it's the universe first, then the dudes, then the dinosaurs, then us!!!

The dude, and the devil, are twins.

And they are both are genius, giving us a dived, in good/evil???

But I, I but can't say a word!!! I don't want too, put out there flame, I'll just have to leave, the choice up to you to choose/decide???

The devil has a poor image team, everything you do, is bad/evil, is it???

I was a 50/50 believer, before I met the dude, it's kinda of strange, he did plan for me to meet him when I was born, it's because he played me the clip, back to me, when I was born, the doctor said "I'm sorry for your son, later on in his life!!!" When handing me over to my mum, I thought he would be, way too busy for me, with so many people dying, on earth!!!

Off topic, this is a health tip, I've come up with/someone told moi or I read when I've come back down here???

Here's 1, due to my???

Laziness, I wanted a way too, cook beef burgers, without

watching them and turning them over and over again!!! When being grilled/cooked.

It came to moi!!!

Steam them!!!

Put them into a metal dish, like bowel, to catch the oil from them, as they cook, well I think??? It's healthier when you eat them???

Why???

You can see, the oil in them, when done cooking them, because, when steaming them, dry heat goes into the burgers, forcing the oil out, as they cook, when done, pour the oil in the bin, or on a used kitchen towel.

That's a load, of oil entering your body, the oil could be animal fat, or veg oil???

And water, from the frozen burgers, another 2, fat ideas???

Came to my broken mind, but I've not tried, them out yet???

1. Is to steam the burgers, for 20 minutes, or longer to make sure, the burgers, are cook through, then add, a slice of cheese, on top of the burger, switch the fire off, put the lid put back on for about a minute??? The heat from the burger and steam, should melt the cheese???

2. If you, hand made the burger??? Just add, grated cheese in with the mix, when cooked, you should have, a melted cheese burger, internally??? NOPE TRIED THAT, AND I FORGOT??? CHEESE IS MADE OUT OF FAT!!! So grilled it'll be then, as the cheese flavour, can't override, the beef taste!!! Kinda cheese burger, well sort of??? Try it yourself, for your own option???

Well I tried, the grated cheese one, and low and behold, cheese is flavoured fat!!!

Because the whole burger cooked forcing the cheese out, so the flavour was left in the meat.

I haven't tried, grilling them, just yet, too get the melted cheese effect, when cooked???

So everything I say, is out there, but I'm stupid enough, to put it all in one place, for you to read!!!

And another thing, to put in with the burgers, is frozen meat dumplings, if brought from a, Chinese supermarket??? If you, want to eat a load of meat and pastry??? It makes the meat dumplings, have a lot of flavour!!! Due to the steaming in the burger oil released from the burgers, slightly better then vinegar used, just my view on flavour, but if you want the sourness??? Go for it, I mean the vinegar, but if meat flavour, is your thing???

Then have them, O natural???

CHAPTER 9

....

They say, drink 8 glasses of water, a day, so that'll be 250 ml X 8 = your 8 glasses for the day, it's to help your body/ system, to flush out the toxins, the best time, they say, is in the morning, before breakfast, they say, you need 3 glasses, of warm water, and its easier, to help, find your vanes, now my messed mind, has come up with, a few ideas, on finding vanes, well the, 1st one, is for a parametric, to give you drugs, or medicine, to get well???

The next thing comes, to mind is, just a bit, wrong??? It's to get, HIGH!!!

O I've slightly changed that, or had new info on it??? It's to have 4 glasses of water in the morning, as breakfast, then can you still, have the recommended 8 glasses a day, or you can have 250 ml X 4 = 1 litre as breakfast, then that makes you, drop 1 large or maybe more large, hey everyone's diet is different!!! I've not timed it, but soon, then wait 45 minutes then eat food, and for the rest of the day, please can you!!! Fit in another 4 glasses of plain water??? Well I don't because I'm a lazy fool!!! Give your body time, to absorb the water, then you'll be ready for more food!!! Eat again/not??? Hey it's your life???

Another thing is, can boiled water, be cooled down, to be drank/consumed??? They say, room temperature is GOOD!!!

It's because, the lime scale, found in British tap water, has been removed, leaving you with, clean water!!!

Because I think???

Lime scale, can give you, kidney stones??? I think??? My thinking goes, as your kidneys, have to, filter out the water, I believe your kidneys, will hold on to some lime scale, hey it's my theory thinking at you???

When you brush your teeth, do you clean or brush your gums as well???

It's from my, broken memory!!!

It goes back to, when I was in, secondary school, I had my front tooth, knocked out in, a game of hockey, I was too stupid!!!

Not to buy gum shields, for my teeth, I didn't know???

I was gambling on, not having my teeth knocked out, I DIDN'T KNOW??? I was a life gambler then, not having a gum shield, too save my teeth from being knocked out.

Well it happened too moi, a friend of mine hit the ball, and the ball, was flying towards my head, then BLAM!!!

Blam, no pain, then I opened my mouth, and my front tooth, just fell out!!!

My tooth, got picked up, and put in a glass of milk, and I was taken too the hospital, where they reinserted my tooth, when the doctor, did it, I was as quite as a mouse, as my tooth, got put back in!!! Then the doctor shook my hand, and I asked him, why???

And he said, I'm a person, who didn't scream!!! When he reinserted, my tooth.

I also had a, plastic top teeth holder made for me as well, it's kinda like a glove, for your top row of teeth, that's when I started to brush my gums, because I couldn't brush my top rack of teeth, so I did my gums then, then a few weeks went by, then I had too go back, to have the teeth shield removed,

I did accedendly remove my teeth shield once, and sniffed it, and it smell it sooo bad!!! But I put it back in, too hold my tooth in.

I think your gums, are a good indicator, for your over all health???

And you only, get 1 set of teeth in life, so look after them, PLEASE!!!

I know teeth, can be replaced, but it's just not the same as real teeth!!! And the feeling you get from real teeth!!! And fake ones, don't feel a thing!!! And they need to be, drown in cleaning fluid, when you go to bed, that means more work for you, at the end of the day!!! (ah NOOOOOOOOOOO)

Like if your gums bleed, you have a very poor diet, and your gums are not being looked after, which hold your teeth in your mouth, and a new theory is, you might develop mouth cancer, because your mouth is, still dirty??? (as this is only a, theory thinking, but if you look at it, from a logical point of view, it kinda makes sense??? Dirty mouth = mouth cancer!!! Who will prove moi wrong??? Unless you hold your mobile phone, next too your gums, while you talk on speaker phone, or run the phone across your jaw line??? And the irony thing is!!! The food you consume, which gives you life!!! Which can also, give you cancer, I know, Ah what to do??? Where to turn???)

Like when you brush the front, or sides of your teeth, do you move your tooth brush up or down a bit, to do you're gums as well, it's a lot easier with an electric tooth brush, if DONE??? You might only see, the dentist, once a year??? I know, they say, see the dentist, twice a year!!!

But if the dentist, says once a year, it's coming from a, professional point of view, from my experience, I ate crispy pork skin, we cooked, our selves, it was a bit too dry, for my family, so most of the skin, was removed from/taken off the pork, so a lot, of dry pork skin, on the side, so I, ate the lot!!!

If that, happens to you??? Can you please, donate, the money you saved, too Brain injury group UK??? But how much??? I could, do the book title, 50/50, but **no**!!! I'll ask for, just £12.00, then you can keep the rest??? As this is, just a book, you've already donated to Brain injury group UK, thank you!!! And you only see the dentist once a year, if still twice every year, then you don't have too!!! Or just once a year seeing the dentist, after reading my method??? So can you please, donate every year, with the money you saved!!! Once or twice, a year, it's your choice??? Just £12.00 once a year, if you see the dentist once a year??? Or £12.00 twice a year??? What am I getting at??? If seeing the dentist twice a year, then don't bother!!!

I'll do some, random maths, for you!!!

If brought, the book at age 30???

Lets just say, you live until 100??? Because we are now!!!

So £12.00 x by 70 years??? = £840.00, if you live that long??? If not??? Still I have too say "a big thank you, from all the people, that attend Brain injury group UK!!!"

I'm not giving you, a guarantee!!! Place into heaven, if you self suicide, I'm giving you, a bargaining chip??? Against the devil!!! Sorry too say, that'll be a, hell no!!! Because he, wants more people to play with!!!

Evilness came, to my mind!!!

Just by touching, the book, it has enlisted, you into, donating to Brain injury group UK, it's because, the devil is a cheeky mofo!!! And he'll do anything, to get your soul!!!

Like I said, I'm kinda working for him!!! Now!!!

CHAPTER 10

· ·

When you, want too???

Or the 18th of December, when I was reborn???

As I said, the magic number is 3!!!

So £3.00, is all I'm asking for, and the rest back to you??? Or you can be, a person with a big heart??? And donate more then £3.00, or just be a robot and donate £3.00??? Every year???

I think??? It's because, you have healthy, gums to hold in, your clean teeth in???

Sorry to say, if you brought, this book, and not donated, to Brain injury group UK???

Then the devil, will get to be, you new dead buddy!!!

Brush your teeth, twice daily, morning and at night, just before you, go to sleep, or an hour before you go to bed??? If you had a, hot drink??? It'll take an hour, for your teeth, to cool back down, to brushing teeth temperature, as the Interweb says??? Or you can, eat a cold apple or drink room temperature water, or try swooshing cold water or ice cold water, around your mouth, 3 times, spit the water out, or drink it??? Hey it's your life, so you can choose??? And you can, also unwind, for the day. When you wake up, go eat your breakfast, due to your body making a sleeping, chemical, to help you sleep better at night, when you had breakfast, go brush your teeth, so you'll be all good for the day, sorry my bad!!! As I've had new info, brush you teeth first then have breakfast!!! But there is a time limit, for that sleeping chemical, and it's 40 minutes, so eat food during that time, if not??? Well I had, 2 hours of sleep that day, I waited an hour and 8 minutes, then food, I'm a curious cat, I wanted to know??? If I was healed or not??? If had breakfast first, if warm wait 33 minutes, for your teeth to cool back down, then go brush them.

That's where the saying, comes from, "breakfast, is the most important, meal of the day!!!" But there is, a time limit, to it, it's yes you've, guesstimated it, it's 40 minutes. (well not so, with anyone, who had a brain injury, well not so for me!?!?!?)

Like having milk, every morning during hay fever season, I think??? Can reduce hay fever, or make it go away, like an old, fairy tale saying, that comes to mee broken mind, it's "poison can, cure poison" know I know, that hay fever, isn't a poison, that can kill you!!! But it, kinda, works on the same principle, and the milk, has to be straight up!!! Not diluted, in tea/coffee, if done??? You'll be drinking, I think??? 1/12th of milk, now that is, too diluted, for it too work well!!! So cereal it is, in the morning, or a glass of milk straight up, during the summer months, or when the pollen season, starts??? Well my theory thinking goes???

Natural honey is, made from plants above the ground, cows eat grass, grown from the ground, so milk produced isn't as good, as honey???

But it takes along time, like 16 years for me??? Because there, are no short cuts in life!!! As I found out.

I've been a car nut, since I was 3 years old, I can't believe, I wanted too be free, that's what driving is too me, freedom!!! And a friend of mine, said that as well, or is freedom to him!!!

CHAPTER 11

....

They say, eat or have an apple, everyday.

Why???

It helps you, drop 1 large everyday, that's the apple skin, and they said why???

The apple skin, helps you intestines to move/exercise, too pass out the food, you have eaten, in the day, too make, more room, in your body, for new food, which gives you more energy.

Well I read, eat 2 apples, a day, to cover, your fruit intake for the day, I'll say???

Have an apple, for breakfast, then you, can choose, when to, eat the other 1???

And also, if you eat, 3 almonds, a day!!!

My sister fashion magazine, said so.

&if you have money, to throw at Actimal, the yoghurt company, well I have had 3 bottles a day, of that stuff, and made moi, drop large, 6 times in 1 day, that's during a 24 hour cycle.

I think this is the only book, I can do, because my mind is just too random, and comes up with bits and bobs, now and again, not enough too, write another book again, but then again, who knows??? If DONE, it'll be, more of my messed up thinking??? But moved on, slightly I think??? So maybe, the same SHIT??? Rehashed at you???

Or it'll be the book of, evil people, on Earth now!!! Or

I go on, BBC world news, and tell the whole world, this person, is pure evil, to rob a, British charity, only thinking??? Of them self, and not helping out, a charity, or the British public now, so you'll, kind of be suing everyone in England.

Evil Den, says no!!! Or a big maybe??? If they, are evil enough, too rob a charity???

I can only leave, the choice, up to the general public, on what, too do??? As we live in the reality of choice.

CHAPTER 12

....

My tuned, Pug (Peugeot) diesel had more torque then my Honda civic.

Honda 116 ft-lb Vs Pug 154 ft-lb of torque, and that's what moves, a car, torque, horse power is only top end speed, you are, never going to reach, that on public roads!!! Well I kinda did, when I had the Pug 306, but it was only, a low top speed, because it's only a diesel (105 mph, on the speedo, well just 100 MPH / 98 MPH then, because the speedo, are suppose to be 10% out, I'm not telling everyone too speed, just random information still stuck in mee broken mind!!!)

My Pug only had 107 bhp, but my Honda had 157 bhp and was a lot faster at the top end, that's a good thing about having a diesel turbo, it gives, you a chunk of torque too use when the turbo is spinning up, and it would out accelerate a car with no turbo, at speed. (I guesstimate???)

I've worked out, why you snack.

It's the devil trying to fatten you up, when you die, because you won't be able, to run away from him, that fast in hell, but the other side of that coin is, it keeps your blood sugar level stable/mellow, only natural foods, work well, junk food turns into fat, because your body, will be confused??? Like what da hell is dat shit, now I'm confused???

Fat it is then for you!!! If your fat, when you die??? You can look back on life, and say I enjoyed eating!!! There is no physical pain, in hell, but it's much worse!!!

Visual pain, images of people you know and love, getting torched in front of you, and you can't stop it, or close your eyes!!!

Due to being dead and no eye lids to close!!!

My random mind went off on one!!!

Why am I half a zombie???

Because, I've got the living dead, part down big time!!!

But not the rotten flesh, that's why half a zombie.

And why is someone I know, having a male period, someone normal calls it depression, well it's a male period, because there is no mess, just pain in the mind!!!

Well the gambler, in moi, says if you suffer, from depression???

I say do a life gamble, 50/50 it'll make your life more interesting, living that way!!! It sure does, when I drove. my car!!!

It's cos my dad he thinks, life is an easy ride, and fate decided to make his life, dam hard for him!!!

He is the main character down here now, I know what you are thinking???

Only good things, happen to them, but this is life, random things, happen to anyone???

CHAPTER 13

I have a fat body, it's not the fat you think it is, but can force the fat out I've eaten in the day, like my pillow has a towel, on it, and it has a yellow tinge on it after a month.

I can't be a Western physiologist, because I'm a mix in Eastern med's as well, just a little thou, so you get the best from both sides, East and Western med's, Western med's, which mainly use pills.

I'm just a random doctor, I don't like, too follow, any books, that's just, way too boring for me!!!

I know it's been, proven by science!!!

But random things, just happen in life!!!

I know the chances are small, like 0.001%

But there always room, for something else to crop up, I really don't have a glue??? (clue???)

I just like to be random!!!

I don't know why, my brother wants life too be easy, and looking at only the bad outcome in life, it will happen, because you've set your mind, to be bad or negative!!!

I see a 50/50 outcome who knows??? As the saying goes, "there are 2 sides, too every story!!!" Or 2 choices in life??? There defiantly are, 2 faces or sides, on every coin!!!

I did take the easy way out, and look what happened to moi!!!

I had to start life again!!! As half a zombie, no rotting

flash, just living dead!!! Or a charming half vampire, NO BLOOD DRINKING!!!

With all the old memories of how I, use to be, as a person!!!

I know after reading this, you'll come up with your own questions to ask me!!!

I can't answer them, but I'll try, too do my best???

Why do I/am I looking after my USB keyboard???

Because it's a gift from Kelvin Li, because I busted my old black, flexible USB keyboard, by leaving it plugged in, and now got a pink one, and I scraped, the black one or I threw it away.

Eat 3 hours before you sleep, or 2 hours cos you need time to digest your food, but you need some food left in your belly too, help you fall asleep well.

Treat your brain like an electric oven, it takes along time for it to cool off, when you sleep at night, they say, you need too, unwind for the day, they say 15 min's, but a sleep expert, says it takes 2 hours to unwind for the day or night, cos your brain, is like a dimmer switch/light, they say, but I say, it's like an, electric oven, cos I'm a fatty!!!

Another way is, too meditate, before you go to bed, they say it helps with, insomnia, if you suffer from that as well??? Not too sure how long??? Just fit it into your 2 hours of unwinding time??? Or do it, for 2 hours??? It helps, set the brain waves, too sleep mode/time.

Then take 15 min's off, the time every night, to sleep well???

I know it's more boring then hell, but the upside to it is, you can sleep better at night.

Sleep is for, the brain, too fix itself

I kinda know why some people can only sleep 5 hours or less, of sleep a night, it's due to them having a bigger brain, and can fix there brain faster at night when they slumber, AKA sleep.

Ear wax, science say it's dirt, I ask why isn't it black??? Like dirt??? I say it's used up omega 3 oil.

But my take on it is, your brain is taking a dump, and the result, is yellow wax in your ear, it's your used brain juices moving around, then forming, into a lump of ear wax.

CHAPTER 14

••

In the French film, called "Taxi" Daniel says "real drivers, are gamblers!!!" And I, use to gamble my, driving licence, on long runs, out of the town, I LIVE IN!!!

Like when Kelvin Li, came to the UK, to go to Lego Land London, I don't remember, but he thought my driving, was CRAZY!!! Because, I drive my car, with a, 50/50 chance or outcome???

Because he's not, a hardcore gambler, he's just a normal person!!!

I'm a lucky fool WHY???

Cause I've got no pain, knocking on my brain!!! And got my taste buds back, after my Acupuncture session!!! I did train, for standing pain, back in secondary school, what do I mean, by train for it??? And my foot doctor said, I must, have a, high pain thresh hold, because, I have, no pain, from a corn on my foot, training was having a dead arm, contest with Ben Chav, (AKA Ben Ch, I can't use his real name, because I've not asked him, anyone in my year, will know him???). It was the first one, who felt pain, gave up, meaning, the other person, won the competition, there was pain, but I just moved it to the side of my brain, and had another punch!!!

It was, the one who ever gave up first, the other person won the competition.

Another saying came to my mind, after a cooking lesson

down in Totton Brain injury group UK, it's good to move your other arm, but another saying, came into my busted mind, it's "move it, or lose it!!!" I know, it's when someone, is standing on there feet, but that also goes for, anyone with a brain injury, because, they've lost the use of there dominate side, of there body, so they have to, use the other side of there body, if they keep on, using that side, of there body??? They'll lose, the former, dominate side, so they have to, move it, or lose it!!!

G.P are only here to give us medical scientific findings.

We got to do, the other half of the medical thing, to get ourself well???

It's a 50/50 thing, them giving you the drugs to get well, then you got to put in the other half, in getting well, for yourself, it maybe boring, but the upside is, you can get, well/better from it!!!

I mean drink lots of water to clean, your body or system, to be cleaned out, science says 2 litres a day.

I can only think, of 1 huge downside, it's being diabetic, you can only slow it down, you can't make your body produce more insulin, all day, for it to be gone for good. (Or can you??? With all natural foods, I think??? That's no use of, salt or sugar??? In it.)

I think, I know, how you become diabetic, both types as well, and maybe, the third type, as well now??? Western med's say, if you don't eat for 3 hours, your blood sugar level will drop, and that's how you get type 2 diabetes, which may lead to hypothalamic now??? It's the same as not eating for along time, if sugar is consumed, maybe just type 2, if not then, type 3, meaning you need sugar now!!! Well another way, to avoid, type 2 diabetics, is too, keep your body busy,

I mean, me, and my sister and Teck Soh, we worked out at the gym, for 3 hours+, and we are, not diabetic now!!! Or another way, is too drink, something sweet, e.g. fruit juice, or do a life gamble, carbonated soft drink, which may lead too, some kinda of tooth decay???

Do I hear, Alan Levi screaming!!!

You diabetic, fools now!!!

I think??? If not eating food, and doing nothing, or not moving the blood in your body around, you'll get type 2, diabetes???

If working out, you are confusing, the body and moving your blood around, your body, it doesn't know what to do???

If you eat??? Then your body will say, food, good!!! If you sleep, it will say time too recharge the body, no diabetes for you, this time round!!!

Eastern med's say it's having too much sweet stuff, that uses up, all the insulin, in your body, that you can produced at that time, and can't keep up with your eating habits, or it's you enjoying too much, sweet stuff or salty stuff now!!! I didn't know that salt, also uses up insulin as well, which can lead to diabetes type 1, then your body says to you, no more insulin, enjoy life that way, my beeatch!!!

Science believes, drinking too much fruit juices, causes type 2 diabetes, but my Eastern med's side says, no it's type 1 diabetes, due to all the sweetness, that use up all insulin, in your body, from the drink!!!

CHAPTER 15

If you've had, a head injury???

You have been removed from the group of "Norm" or normal people.

But!!!

I still don't!!!

Because I've, not done the research into it, it'll still be a hell no!!! To that, because, my niggar, doesn't want you, to live, that way!!! Making life 1 sided!!! Everything is sooo sweet in life = enjoying yourself, too much.

They say eat breakfast, within 40 minute's of waking up, it's because your body produces a sleeping chemical, to make you sleep better/quicker, at night??? Well quicker, in my, experience??? And my mum too!!! Well if I do that, I get 2 hours of sleep, or 1 hour of sleep at night, the same with 4:30 hours, I did try 2:48 min's, and still the same result, so now it's an hours before I eat breakfast??? Or was, now it's, drink water, then wait, 45 mins then eat fruit, for breakfast or overnight oats???

Martin Stark on Spire FM, wonders??? Why do you take a shower before you go for a swim, after having been in the sauna or steam room???

Now do you stand at the side of the pool, and take a leak into it??? I mean do you urinate, into the pool???

That's what you are doing, if you don't shower, because

I think your sweat is $1/12^{th}$, made up of your urine or pee pee???

Well an American lad, who died and came back, to Earth, he says heaven is real!!!

It's a 50/50 thing to moi, yes it's real!!!

But, not physically real!!!

Meaning, your physical body, can't enter that realm!!!

I call it the waiting room, and he can't remember the book, we all have, and seeing how his life could of turned out???

Like I'm back to tell yee all, how brain cell are made, it is a work of art the brain.

Think of it this way, the brain is, like a big lump of gum, in your head, it implodes to create, a line in your brain, which we call, a brain cell.

I think the brain, is kinda a limitless place, to store information, when the information is used by your body, your body, gets rid of the cell, in your urine, that's why, your urine is dark yellow, when alcohol is consumed, it kills your brains cells, then they are dead brain cells leaving your body.

We all know alcohol, kills brain cells, in Hong Kong, they did an experiment, drinking too much alcohol, can lead to old timers decease, aka Dementia, it's because a small amount, of alcohol is left in the brain, the body can get rid of the alcohol, with your blood moving it around, and the heat, your body can produces, but your brain, cannot, so alcohol is left in your brain!

Like I said there are 3 ways in getting Dementia, the whole brain is one big mussel, it can create new brain cells everywhere, in the brain, if the brain is over worked, damaged or drenched in alcohol, it loses the ability to create new brain cells.

My thinking of getting dementia is...

1. Is being too old.

2. Brain damaged.

3. Alcohol

4, Over use of brain, meaning brain cell created, but then lost quickly.

CHAPTER 16

How do we get, dementia???

Dementia is, having trouble, taking down new information, giving/spoken to you.

Well 2 things come to my broken mind, 1 is hortatory, 2 is over worked brain, that's also goes for old age for you, because in this day and age, we need to learn new things to keep up, with the moving times, and that is telling are brains, to create new brain cells, if your brain is over worked, it decides not to create any more, new brain cells, for you.

There is, away around it, but NOT, in Britain, they have put in a law, some form of GBH (Grievous Bodily Harm), in using long needles to reach the pressure point in are bodies to fix the problem, is illegal, I'm on about Acupuncture, he knew, we would wear out, are brains, or have an accident, to loose the ability, to create new brain cells, and he gave us the knowledge to fix, ourselves, it's called Acupuncture.

Sleep is your brain, saying to you, I need to be fixed, so sleep, my niggar!!!

If you've had a brain injury???

You'll most likely, have neurological fatigue, I think??? The first person too have it, was, Leonardo da Vinci, because he sleeted, every 4 hours, he said it was to recharge, his intelligence, but, I'm a theory man, that's the same as, Neurological fatigue, when you wake up, 1 hour or so, fatigue kicks in again, having my Acupuncture sessions, in

Hk, has cured that!!! I don't have enough, money, too keep my treatment going, every 6 months, I wish!!! So now it's a yearly trip, to Hong Kong, that's why, I want to bring, the cure to Britain!!!

When your brain, and body is all fixed, or charged up, it'll say time, to get up and do some damage on the world/ Earth, NOT BLOWING THINGS UP!!! Just be a fool!!! Or just be normal!!!

I've come up with 2 ways of getting diabetes, and maybe, the third type now??? And now the third type, which is you, needing sugar too keep your blood going.

First one has Eastern med's in put, and that is consuming to much sweet/salty foods, because you need your body, to produce a lot of insulin, to balance it out, it's what insulin is, too keep your body well balanced/mellow, that's type 1 diabetics.

And type 2 is based on Western med's, they say you need to eat food every 3 hours, so your blood sugar levels, does not drop, to nothing, another easier way, to avoid, type 2 diabetes, is too have a sweet drink, but not, too sweat of a drink!!!

So you, don't get, type 1 diabetes.

Well I think??? It's, pure irony, my parents, have type 2 diabetes now, and they use to own a restaurant, meaning, easy access, to food, so why type 2 diabetes now??? Well my dad, started off, with type 1, because, he consumed, too much salty foods, then moved on too type 2 diabetes now, it's down to his eating habits, food at 5 pm, then work at the restaurant, when finished working, lets say, he ate at 00:28 am, now that's 7 hours without food, with general walking and lifting plates, not moving the blood around in your body, no wonder why type 2 diabetes now.

Sugar and salt, is a double edge sword, as they both, need insulin, to be made natural, for your body, to process it.

If over done??? Then it will slice you and dice you, for life!!! With type 1 diabetes, as sugar and salt, both need insulin, to be diluted, for your body to process it!!!

But I hear you say, "sugar is, so sweet!!!" "we need that, pick moi up NOW!!!"

I think??? Natural sugar, is OK, but please don't add, anymore, to the natural sweetness!!!

If both parents, are diabetic, there child, won't be!!! If the parents, developed it, later on in life???

It's down to the child choice in food, will they follow there parents, eating habits or not???

The child can, start fresh, in life, will they follow, there parents eating habits or not???

CHAPTER 17

....

Well I think???

It's more like 3:30, because your body, isn't a light switch, on/off??? Cos your insulin, will linger for a bit longer, then it's all gone, at 4 hours, I think???

I have a greed, for flavours, when I eat food, I like to experience, more then one flavour in my mouth, like I like, having a bacon, tea roll, you get salty and sweet, in one bite, that also goes for having pineapple and chicken vindaloo/lamb vindaloo, you get sweetness from the pineapple, then a kick of hotness from the vindaloo, how awesome, is that???

Is there anything on the market, that offers, spicy and sweet???

And, a hot drink I made up, it's a chino mocha tea, it's add 1 tea bag in it/too the mocha chino, so make a mocha, then add 1 cappuccino and tea bag, I've just shorten the name of it, now that drink confuses my brain??? Or a new way, shown to me, is too make the tea first, let it brew for 5 minutes, then pour the tea into the cappuccino, and then add the instant coffee, and maybe the hot chocolate, I leave the choice in your hands???

It's like, what is it???

Coffee or tea or cappuccino???

It sure is, a lot of caffeine!!! I didn't know, if you suffer from ADHD, caffeine makes you tired, I've had ADHD, since 14, because I had near enough, a pint of coffee, or I left, 1 cm too move the glass about, when I finished working at Chef Peking, being a dish washer, because of my age.

The bad point, in doing all that, is losing your, fine detailed, taste buds, you still, have your main taste buds, E.G. salty and sweet.

I'm too wearied??? Or am I, still broken???

Now it does a, catch 22 on me, makes me tired at first, then 20-30 minutes, down the line, the caffeine kicks in, like a, bat out of hell!!! Then I'm wired/really active???

All that, caffeine in it, I'm still feel like, a mellow fool??? I don't run up walls, backwards, even thought, I should be able too, with all that caffeine in me!!!

It's because, I'm still broken!!!

Or back when I worked at Chef Peking, at the end of the night, I had the left over coffee, I didn't know how much it'll be??? So I got a pint glass, and poured the coffee in it??? No ALCOHOL ADDED TO IT!!! So I could drive, or I wasn't old enough for alcohol??? I know, what you are thinking??? It's a family business, so why not, get someone else, too drive home??? I have ONLY JUST FOUND OUT!!!

That caffeine is, also an, relaxing chemical!!!

So gets you wired!!! But claims you back down after 30 mins??? It's another 50 50, due to the fact, I know, it kicks in or gets you wired, after a 20 min rest, then all *&!! =£$%^£ like a bat out of a warm place??? Then 30 mins later, your be a mellow, fool again???

Like I said, I get no pleasure, from drinking alcohol, but do from driving a car.

And went home, and had a shower and still went to bed, about an hour later, I guesstimate??? That'll be kinda true, as the caffeine has worn off/I gone home to bed, like moi!!!

It's why we are alive, do you have a taste, for life??? Well there are 2 versions, in my busted world, 1 is to, go out there and try different foods and drinks, making life more interesting to live it, because you don't need to eat when you are dead!!!

Or am I, a gluttony for punishment??? Looking for pain, to feel alive???

As I have a 50/50 mind, porn isn't all bad!!!

The other side to it is, getting to see someone naked, and you didn't, have to pay them, to be naked for you, just buy the video, the other thing that came to my mind is, he gave us porn, it's the devil who made it evil, but I can't say why or how!!!

All I can say is, it became evil, in the 1940's, was there porn then??? Well that'll be, a BIG NO!!! Because, as there was no video technology back then, FOOL!!! Or they had photo porn, naked people!!!

CHAPTER 18

The devil and THE DUDE, both watch PORN!!!

They both decide, to not make the woman, go through pain, that's why we have cream pie clips, or scenes, we know, in science, sperm to egg = baby and it'll, destroy, the porn industry!!! If the female actress, got pregnant in it!!! Because the devil, doesn't want the woman, to go through pain!!! So he gets 1 person, to go to hell, to keep him happy, so it won't be, full of hand outs to him!!!

I didn't know???

They used a sponge, to stop the seamen, from entering the fallopian tube, to the egg.

And they, don't want to destroy, the porn industry, with girls, who had a toy, up there ass, and then put it into, there pussy, because the toy is still dirty, even after sucking it dry!!!

All I can say is, start fresh, so get a brand new toy.

He'll rather let, married couples, have children, then they are, the dudes children, and he'll make them choose, the good/bad route in their life???

As I said, we live in, the choice of reality???

He doesn't, want both of the parents, forcing the child to be evil, so they go, down to hell!!! If we are the dudes, children, then the devil, just doesn't want hand outs to hell!!! It's more interesting for him, if we choose, to go down to hell, then he'll play, that clip back to them or us, when we/ they are down in hell.

Cos we know in science, sperm to egg = child, they both play the X factor, on who gets a child??? And the sex of the child, Cos they want to, know if, they'll get more chicken, to eat??? From there offspring??? Or NOT???

Well it's what, I think???

The dude, made blonds, have a problem with there brain, we call them, being blond, well the actual sickness is called Dementia, they have a problem remembering new stuff, which is also known as Dementia, but we call it, being blond!!!

I mean blonds, are good to look at, my point of view, first plus point, and if they have a brain, to match, then they win, win all round, and that's unfair, to the rest of US!!!

It really annoys too me, people who walk on the road, following the traffic, are they made out of steal/metal??? And as fat, as a car??? Or big as a bicycle??? And you are, putting all your trust, in the driver???

It would be alright, if they were doing it for, a voluntary suicide, putting all your trust, in the driver, as they say, "shit happens!!!" Do you want to find out, that's why you do a hardcore gamble??? No money, is involved, that's why it's a hardcore gamble!!! You have to walk, against the traffic to be safe, because it's down to this being, a visual reality, if you see the driver and the driver see you, you make eye contact, so they'll avoid you, and the same with them!!!

Why do general cyclists, not wear helmets??? I know, it's quicker and easy not too!!! Can you see, the future??? That's why no need for a helmet???

And you look cooler, if you don't have 1 on, like I said "SHIT HAPPENS?!?!?!"

I think??? I may still have memory problems now, I guesstimate??? I'm still tired everyday, even after sleeping, which is called, Nero logical fatigue, that's why, we are fatigued, it's are brain trying, to create more or new brain cells, is my speech still poo or poor??? Well I do, speak too foreigner, in Sub way, to order mee food, and they seem to understand moi, and the bus company, in Salisbury, they understand moi too.

Well this is, a link to YouTube, of moi speaking about Brain injury group UK, the video was done for, brain injury week back in May of 2015, and my speech was poor back then, due to moi(me) not speaking much, I don't seem to talk much after my accident or before it, because now I found out, I'm an introverted thinker, here's the link address.

https://www.youtube.com/watch?v=ome28JwPYb8

I also did, my biscuit poetry, for Brain injury group UK in the Southampton/Totton link, to a bunch of solicitor down in Totton.

I think??? They understood moi, because, I cracked a joke, at the end of my performance, and they did laugh at it or was that just moi, or I can't tell a joke???

O yeah, I would like to, thank Kelly Clarkson, for filling in the time, up to my accident, you were chosen, to give him a plug, when you won, the American X factor, can I use your name, and him to give both of you a free plug???

Can I add respect, has to be earned, it doesn't come, from fame or with the money you make!!!

He says, it's all good, giving him a plug and her???

I did ask you for your permission, to use your name, on

Fatbook AKA Facebook, but you blocked moi, cos I said some random things to you first, then you blocked moi, dam good move!!!

You took the easy way, out of life!!!

The devil, gave us the easy way out, in are life's, like self suicide, you will, go down to see him,

Do you want, that too happen??? Then the pain starts for you, for entirety??? Because you took the easy way out, then he, he'll gets to play with your soul for eternity, showing you the choice, that brought you too him, now your new album, the title is up your own ass, just my option on it... Or believing, in your own skills, you have in yourself???

As your famous, you think???

That respect, is yours for free!!! As they say, you have to earn respect, sorry to say, you cannot, earn it now!!!

You didn't even give moi, a minute, of your time, to tell moi, to shut up, and go to hell!!! You wearied O!!! And before, you go to hell!!! Please, can you please, not message moi anymore!!!

I would of taken that, under advice, to moi!!!

Telling moi not too, message you!!!

I would of done that!!!

Because you gave me a minute, of your time!!!

And if you said, not too message you!!!

Well maybe 1 or 2 more???

But I can't anymore!!!

You thought, I'll turn it around, and make money off your ass!!!

Well with a 50/50 mind it is, yes for Brain injury group UK!!!

But also, a BIG FAT NO!!!

Because that's your view on me!!!

I'll have to, live with that!!!

I'll just take it as, water off a ducks back, next please!!!

Something came to play, back in the 1940's, and that has, sealed your fate or soul, with him!!!

The album, is called "invincible" meaning you believe in your own skills, no help needed, from my niggar (the dude), why is he my niggar now??? It's because, he sent moi back to eat fried chicken!!! Because he loves it too!!! it's because, he plays that little voice inside are heads!!! Cos he can decide where your money goes, in your pocket, to chicken it up or not???

Now I guesstimate???

That album, will be a big flop??? Or maybe not as I'm giving you a plug???

With no help from him, as we all act for him, he can chose, how we act, for him, I know the things, I say is, hearse and not nice!!! But that's just broken moi!!!

I guesstimate???

Give him a plug, which you have done!!!

&give your money out, to help other people???

To stay on Earth, to entertain him more???

It's why I'm back, it's my brain, having a normal day, it's just being 50/50, it's more interesting for him too, watch moi, it's will I, or won't I die, from the stupid choice, I've just made, or will this, be published or not???

I think??? It will, to see, if I get, mee pants, sued into next week/NOT???.

I can't say what will happen to you, because this is, a book of theorise???

After my accident, somebody told moi, life is made up

of choices, you and I make??? I cannot, undo them, choices that we made??? Or you made, and that also, goes out to all my friends, or former friends???

But my goal, is to be independent, having no one, to relay on, or ask for help.

Smoking and drinking, are great devil toys, drinking is the devils blood, because he wants to make you feel like a vampire, only drinking at night, and thinking, your invincible, that's why you pick fights, with other drinkers, then gives you a hang over, when it's morning, and you just don't want to go out into the sun!!! Smoking is, sucking on the devils cock!!! Or I call them, cancer sticks!!! He is, cumin in you every time you suck on the, cigarette. They both, give you, pleasure when doing it, if you do, die from it??? It'll send you, straight down to HELL, because they both are self suicide items, then the pain starts, because you had the fun, drinking the liquid or inhaling the smoke, then the pain starts for you, for eternity!!!

I feel like standing up, for mother nature.

In the news there was a female, 18 year old, and she sued someone, for raping her, as a child???

Do you not use, monthly rags aka sanitary towels, or tampons??? Because that's a child too moi.

Because Mother nature, says your body, is old enough, to support a child.

18 = adult

That also goes down to, consent, from both parties, as you are both are 18+

It'll just be plain rape, as you are both 18+

Because now, most things have been classed, as legal at 18 years old, in the UK.

If you wanted to, make easy money???

The only thing, that comes to my, busted mind, is porn or teen porn, because your still 18, not hit twenty yet, your still classed as a teenager, at that age, and the age of 19 years old.

Are you naturally, bold as an eagle, down below???

Not hit puberty yet???

Why do we, have cream pie sense's???

Well the thing that comes to my, broken mind is???

The devil doesn't want, hands out to hell!!!

And making the girl go through pain as well, so he gets, one life!!!

Too keep him happy, and it'll destroy the porn industry as well!!!

You don't have to use, monthly rags then???

That is a child to me, not hitting puberty, mother nature, says your body, is not old enough, or developed enough yet, to be able to support a child yet!!!

And she made our, bodies dam smart too!!!

They say chew, after every meal! Or get some chewing gum???

But the only downside to is, your saliva, is still in food burning mode, because chewing food, meaning, your saliva is in food burning mode, so it'll still erode away your enamel, found on your teeth, because your body is still thinking, food in mouth, and needs to be burned down!!!

Or I've put a time limit, on chewing gum, or chewing it, it's for 30 min's, then spit out the gum.

I've read, another downside to, chewing gum is, leading to poor sleep, or hip mussels, not working well!!!

It's to do, with having, a lot of tension, in your jaw mussels.

O yeah, 1 last thing is, we can travel, back in time!!! And to other dimensions/realities, but not in this reality, the universe says, the same matter, cannot be in two, places at once!!!

And if possible, then hell would be, empty!!!

Because the people there now, would leave, and join this reality, cos it's better then hell!!! Or is it???

CHAPTER 19

....

Can an alcohol and water engine, be made??? I think??? If olive oil, was added to the mix, it might replace diesel fuel??? Then it'll be all, natural fuel, but the coldness will freeze, the water used, but it won't freeze the alcohol, can boiled water, or bottled water be used, because there is, no lime scale in there, which can clog, the water ways up, or fuel lines up.

Ah another 50/50 for you!!!

Well my idea started off, back in 2003, when I thought, of using alcohol, to run the engine, then I added water to the mix, since I came back down here!!! It's to stretch it out, and it'll be, more natural then, it'll be a 50/50 mix, during the summer months, then neat alcohol, during the winter months.

It's down too, the fact, alcohol, is like petrol, I also heard on the news, on the 3/9/15, I heard on the news, someone drank petrol, because, it acts like alcohol, it catches fire easily, if mixed with water, will it go further, will 10% of alcohol, mix with water, will that, still work in the engine??? And you, have to be 18, to fill up your car then, and drive because, you are purchasing alcohol, for your car to drink, or run you home too sleep???

But the only downside, too alcohol is, it's 12% down on power vs petrol, but can titanium engines be made??? As titanium is, 45% lighter then steel, so weight saved, = more engine power???

Another idea, is too, put fan generators over the, heating radiators, so wind can give you some power back, I was thinking???

1 in each conner, so you get a bit of wind power, back from moving the car, another idea is, to put tubes in the middle, of the radiator with fans in the tube, collecting the wind movement, but the other thing is, the wind will be lass dense, due to it being heated up??? My ideal set up, would be 8 fans on the top and bottom, 3 fans on the top and bottom, and also fans on each side, making it, an unbroken fan circuit.

But now, I've given myself, a catch 22, the extra weight added to the car.

If my idea worked???

You may, only fill the car up, once a year??? That's far off thinking for you!!! Lets just say, "a monthly trip too the pumps??? A bit more plausible, for you???

And the other+ thing is, it'll be all natural fuel then, there might be a, rise in stainless steel exhausts, due to them, not corroding, from the water, coming out from the engine/exhaust.

As I've seen a video, methanol added to petrol, the only down side is, water found in the methanol, which will lead to a quicker, broken engine as water is bad for the metal engine. I think???

I have a, VERY DANGEROUS WAY, to take the water out of the methanol, well come too think about it???

I think it'll be alright, if a container made??? The methanol poured into a metal container, heated up too 103 c, as water will turn into steam at that temperature, so then you'll be left with, 100% pure methanol!!! I think???

It'll be the new source of fuel for engines, still O natural engine tho???

Will anyone try my idea out??? As I'm back, I think outside the box, as they say!!!

Then you'll still have fuel grades, on how much the methanol is treated or water added, 100% is like super unleaded, 100% methanol add a 10% of water, that should be our normal unleaded petrol we have now???

I think??? If my engine made???

I was thinking of???

All the car manufactures, a 12.5% back to moi, it's too help out an English charity, and the NHS now, and it's too give you the choice, in what brand of car you own???

I don't want the car, to go as there is no more, dinosaurs bones, to run them or to fuel them up with!!!

I would like it, too work in the, rotary engine, or wankel engine, as it's been said, they drink standard fuel, like water!!! (roughly 20+ mpg???)

If my idea, worked on that engine??? It'll be raining, a lot more everyday!!! Because, the amount of water you'll be using to run your car, to get you to places to go???

The other thing is, can more electric cars be made??? Then the fuel will, be all natural from the sun, giving us light and energy.

If my, idea worked???

Could it, be brought into, motor sport???

A good driver, can set a good lap time, of xx:xx, on 50% of alcohol. Then add more water, to reduce the power output of the motor, can they still set a good time, or near there good time???

Then more focus, will be put on, aerodynamics then??? And driver skill???

Give the smaller teams, more alcohol, in there engines, so they can lead, the race with bigger or well known names, are chasing them down!!!

We'll be driving a GREEN CAR, if an alcoholic, engine was up front, an electric motor/engine was in the back, you'll use, the electric motor, for town driving then flick a switch, for long runs, where you need the extra power/speed, 0-28 mph, is for town driving, then 30+mph, alcoholic engine takes over.

Now do you, need extra weight, from carrying the alcohol about???

Can the wheels, charge the electric motor up??? And the heat made, from the breaks, when breaking, can that be turned in to energy??? To give you, a little bit more electric power??? Too charge the electric motor up???

The law should be, more harder, on the person, because, they are drinking, the engine fuel, for them to get home, to sleep, 1 unit is £1000 fine, 2 units is £2500, and 3 units is the magic number, a ban, for 6 months, and a £5000 fine.

I think??? The same should, go for answering a mobile phone, if the call not taken then, will you die on the spot???

Do you feel talkative or thirsty, for alcohol now???

Or water, the better choice!!! You need 2 ltrs, or 3 ltrs, of water a day, if you can drink that much??? A day, that's what science says, you need 2 ltrs a day, but 3 ltrs, if you work out as well??? Well lets just say??? You'll start the day off, with 1 litre of water in the morning, then all you have left is 4 glasses during your day??? So much easier that way. Can you drink 250 ml, every hour??? Times that by 8 or 4 now??? Then you have had your 8 glasses of water, you need everyday, or 2 ltrs, that you need, and can you drink the water slowly, to give your body time, to absorb it, if drunk quickly, you'll need to go to the toilet, more often, it's your body getting rid of the water in you, or ice cold water, makes your body, use energy, to make the water warm, so you kinda burning fat, the slow way round, but the other side of the coin is, your body will try, to match the temperature, of the liquid, you just swallowed, either cold or hot???

I know, it's either crazy or pure insanity??? Because, it doesn't follow logic!!!

But when sweating or hot, you need to have a warm drink of water or something warm, it's for your body to match the temperature, it is at.

But your logical brain or mind says, you need a cold drink, to cool the body back down, but that's only the outside of your body, when the liquid goes in the body, it'll try to match, that temperature, see it's another catch 22, for you, ah!!!

Well I did try that again, and it didn't work this time round!!! That well, but you can you drink, the liquid down quicker thou!!!

So it's a cold drink, that will work, better because, it'll cool down your logical brain down, and you down!!!

I'm kinda lazy and don't drink 2lts of water a day, or I need everyday, but I'm back to bring help, to all my readers???

Or have a drink, that'll help you, fight off the flu, or the cold??? But it needs, to be spaced out, like 3 days, if summer time or everyday, during the winter months.

Get a mug, it's juice/squeeze 1 orange, and 1 lemon, and add 3 tea spoons, of cider vinegar, add boiled water, not boiling hot!!! To the mix, then let it cool down, I choose 12 mins, then use a straw, to drink it down, it'll by pass your teeth, so they won't erode away, with the vinegar in it, because, we all know, acid, erode away teeth, which is the main part of vinegar.

If eroded away slightly???

Try swooshing your mouth out, with a tea spoon full, of coconut oil, just move the oil, about in your mouth, move it around, for about, 10-20 minutes, they say, do this, 4-7 times a week??? Then spit out, the used oil, into the bin!!! Not the sink, unless you are wealthy enough, to pay a plummier, to unclog the drain??? Do this in the morning, before breakfast or brushing your teeth, on an, empty stomach.

They also say doing this, can also whiting, your teeth as well, O yeah can you, go too the gym, and work out for 48 min's??? It's due too, your mouth absorbing the coco nut oil, you aren't drinking it???

But your mouth will still absorb it, meaning it go to your heart, to be clogged up with oil.

Another thing you can do, if you want, to fight the flu or cold off, is to swallow, ginger slices whole, or after it been used, in cooking food, I know what, you are thinking???

But it's lost, all of the goodness, in it!!! Or the goodness, has been used up?!?!?! Or has it???

I think???

It has a wee bit left, in it???

Then your, stomach, can finish the ginger, off!!!

Actually, come to, think about it, it's my get out of jail card, WHY, do I say that???

Because my sister, use to call moi, random D man or just D man or just D, cos I, would just do, random things or odd things, that was before my brain injury, but now I have, had a brain injury, I can, put my blame on that!!!

Another nick name was or is, easy going D/Den.

I don't know how or why!!!

I can turn, the other cheeky, or let things go, it's like if you get annoyed, by the person, annoying you, they win, but if you smile at them, they'll think??? You've lost it or you win, cos you, can take, the higher road, or ground in life!!!

And you, didn't sink, too there level???

But I still don't!!! Why should I, put my blame on an injury, that happen to moi??? That's taking the easy way out of life, but I don't, like to take, the easy way out of life!!!

Because life, isn't an easy ride!!!

It's more fun, to be challenged, like this brain injury, is a challenge for moi, to overcome, not quite done just yet!!!

Still need to go, or do some other thing, or more things in life???

They say, "real men, can take criticism", it's like, water off a ducks back, to moi, I hear it, but I don't like too, keep on thinking, about it!!!

Everything I've said, it'll be like the title, 50/50, will it work for you/not??? Well it did, work then for me, and is still working for moi now, O no, I've been returned, back as a human robot, I did have time limits, that I had to stick too, but not anymore, because I'm kinda, back to normalish, now???

I'm back, to enjoy myself, & have a laugh, while I'm here again.

So should, you!!!

Another tip, for you, if you suffer from, dementia??? Which most likely you don't???

But if you do??? Can you at night, look over what, you have the next day??? So you set, your mind, to what needs to be completed the next day??? Like an hour before you go to bed???

O no!!!

I've given you a, 50/50 choice, on what to do in your life???

Like I said earlier on, in the book unwind for 2 hours, or meditate???

But I've just told you, to set the monkey off in your noggin/brain, if you suffer from, dementia???

It's your life, so please choose???

As Motor neuron decease, sound a bit like, they've had a brain injury, but they have overworked there brain!!! That's why, they lose, the grip of their hands, there brain is saying, no more, work from me, my beeatch!!!

Meaning, no more, new brain cells, created for you!!! Or the use, of your good side, of your body!!!

I think???

I can/could I, bring the cure, to Britain???

But, it'll not happen!!! Because like I said, there is a law, that has been, put in place, for you or them, not to be cured!!!

When dead, you can look back on life, and say, I had fun my niggar!!!

If I, get sued, by anyone???

I've got a, dam good, gift for you!!! You can't come back, to tell anyone!!!

See, it's that dam good!!! It's still, a 50/50 thing, but you know the results, if done???

It's life!!! The choices, we have made, it's like time, only one way, or one direction!!! We or I can't change it!!!

Even with, all the devils children, aka money, we cannot, take anything back!!! Because that's, this reality, and we go to another one, when are time is done down here, in this physical realm!!!

We can't, take back, what we said, or done, we just got too, live, with the choice we made.

Someone said to moi, you are religious, if you believe in my niggar, I say OK, it's your view on life, but my version is, you have to show everyone, that you believe by, going to his house & partying it up every week!!!

As I said, I'm a theory man, only the, afterlife thing are, a big maybe???

That's why, I'm back, to stir thing up, or ruffle, some feathers in this life, that also goes out to, Phil Pimpdaddy Southgate, aka Philip James Southgate, I did ask, for his business details, but nothing from him, on FaceBook, he only had, a head on crash, in a drag race, not as mayor as a brain injury, we kind of cause, controversy, in the things we say or do, in are life, without us, this reality would be so boring, everyone staying safe and normal!!!

Do you, want to die, with a perfect body???

If mutilated or scared???

When dead, you can look back on life, and say, "I sure had a, good time on earth!!!"

The brain facts, are real, because, I living proof of it!!!

I leave you, with the choice, to make??? Will it be, good/bad/the ugly, sorry to refer to a film title, I mean, is it evil???

O yeah, another last thing, GOD is good, GOD is great and GOD is, evil too!!!

Because, he's also helping, out his brother, by giving him, more people to play with!!! That's getting more souls, to play with, is that, a good thing or bad thing???

We share the evil knowledge, about a person back on earth, because it's the choice, that they made, in this life!!! Doing something, that came into play, back in the 1940's.

The devil, is a pure evil, genius!!!

Making his toys, costing you money, too buy!!!

Good bye & good night, to all my, readers???

CHAPTER 20

....

BOO, IF STILL READING???

O no, I've turned you, into a curious cat, want or needing to know my out come???

I need too, put my, foot down, and say it's done!!! If not, you'll, never get to read this, because there is no finishing line, for moi, just keep on going!!!

Now it seems like, we always, needed too be connected, with what's going on around us!!!

Please.

Can you, please turn off/switch off, your electrical device, too be charged, I know you can turn it, or use flight mode/profile, to be charged.

But it does, make the screen, or system, fix itself, if turned off, haven't tried, AMOLED, just yet???

Now that I have, it's one, big ass of a joke!!!

28% more juice, in 5 hours!!!

Not even fully charged!!! In that time!!!

Another way I found out is, too put the device, into power saving mode, then the results are quicker then.

But having the, device, turned off, does charge it quicker!!! And it'll be charged up too 100% when done.

I have tried, AMOLED now!!! And it's still faster and better, too switch off the device!!! But you'll wear out the battery much quicker, ahhh what too do??? It's your life, so you choose please???

I'm also, doing a hardcore gamble on, Alan Levi, Martin Stark, Doyal Brunson, Kelly Clarkson and Madonna???

Being American, is it your culture, to sue moi??? I also know, your whole nation, feed my niggar, with chicken, but the ironic thing is!!! Suing someone, means, you also are, working for the devil!!! I'll have too wait, to find out the answer now, for moi???

Not Alan Levi or Martin Stark, because they are Brits!!! But if you, like to make easy money, like the Americans, in suing moi, but who knows???

I'll tell you, the good and bad points, of suing moi???

Live like a King, or queen, for 12 years, or more??? Now you'll see, the century mark!!!

When done, it'll be HELL for you, for eternity, I can only leave the choice up to you??? Because the devil, gave us, the easy way out, in this life!!!

If Kelly Clarkson, done it???

Sorry too say, it'll be, hell for you, cos my niggar, will be looking out, for his twin.

I did ask, Alan Levi, but he wanted, moi to do more work for him, and not to do a, hardcore gamble, on mee, broken brain??? And not give him a free plug, if you come, and visit Salisbury, and buy/purchase some legal high, or drugs, from him???

Doyal Branson's not on Fb, even tho, I did ask him???

Kelly Clarkson, well, she blocked moi, on FaceBook, as I said, some poor/random things to her, but nothing bad, (well nothing, bad from my, broken brain, or point of view!!!) to her, like I said, it's mee brain, having a normal day!!! She prejudged moi, thinking I was, a normal wearied O, but she didn't know??? I'm a broken fool!!!

Or I've sent back, too Write this story, and help both of them out!!!

Can I mention, Honda, Mazda and Peugeot???

My idea, is open to all car manufactures, but only for a, 12.5 % return, for my idea, why do I offer my, idea to everyone???

Ah, I've given you, another 50/50 choice

Because, the spice of life, is variety, it'll be, soooooooooooo boring!!! If only 1, car manufacturer, only made the engine, and you only had, that make, of car too drive, and it'll take longer, too make the world, a greener place to live in.

Do you want too, join the devil??? Because there is, lots of room for, you too join him!!! And the money you made, from my busted ass, and disable people, who attend Brain injury group UK, and the NHS now, the money from moi, can't pay him to stop, torching you!!!

I know the outcome, will you go and see him now???

I was thinking???

You can have, 3+ types of fuel, first off, is just beer, I know that's low alcohol, then spits like, vodka and brandy, then the last one is, absinthe, is that 60%+??? (from mee broken memory)

As being, famous and rich, you think that everyone, has to respect you!!!

Because you can, buy their ass!!!

But respect has to be earned, no money needed, it's an emotion, that is earned!!!

Now do you win!!!

And charity loses, also being the, evil people, too rob a charity???

I leave the choice, up too you, to decide??? As this is the choice, of reality???

I've picked a stupid time, to release my story!!! Or have I???

As hay fever season has just gone, or has it??? If you suffer from, hay fever??? It maybe gone, in the year 2033, if you follow, my guide??? And if your body is, as broken as mine??? As they say???

Best out of 3, or the magic number is, 3???

Another memory, from secondary school, comes to mee broken mind!!!

Wash and dry, your hands well!!!

Then there is, no moisture left, to move the dirt around/ body dirt, aka dead brain cells!!! Found in your pee pee or urine.

Sunny Chan, has given me, knowledge into, are mother tongue, or the first language, you learn at school, that stays with you your whole life, then you add more languages or other languages, on top of your mother tongue, he has also shown me, you have got too have, the need to learn new things in life, to be able to, survive.

As he learnt to Write Chinese, and speak Cantonese, at school, then moved to Oz, he picked up English, it's the opposite to me, and I know, simple François, aka French, that I remember, from secondary school, and other random junk, or other languages, I've pick up in this life!!!

CHAPTER 21

I don't know why, this came too mee broken mind???

It's kinda of, left field to you!!!

It's too be able too, move radiation about???

I think??? As everything, in life, can be move, or transferred, I was thinking??? Moving radiation about, or turning it into a physical form??? As radiation, will never go blow sea level, just stay on top of water!!!

I was thinking??? Spraying water on or around radiation, I think the water particles, will trap the radiation in it??? Then you'll have radioactive water, I was thinking??? Run the water, through a water filter, to then turn, the radiation into a physical form???

Woman, who have had, breast implants, are asking the devil, to make them more attractive, or make them self feel better??? I think it's the devils, boogies, because that's the only thing, too leave the devil, that is apart of him.

I'm not, gay, or am I???

If you go back to the old, use of the word, gay, meaning "happy"

Well I'm like the book title, 50/50.

Now the use of gay, is a homo sexual, man or woman, but it depends, on when you, where brought up??? With that saying??? Or now it means, gay man now!!!

I think??? Having a foreskin, is like Jesus, because, my

niggar, wanted his son, too feel the full pleasure, of using his third leg!!!

Jesus had one, because he was the first man to be documented, in this reality, he had the lot!!! Then a few, century's went by, then the devil, thought???

I'll take that, pleasure away!!! From my sheep/actors.

Then no more, foreskin, for us!!!

I know Jews, made it a tradition, to circumcise, there boys, meaning there giving, there boys, the touch of the devil!!! And the ironic, thing is, they follow GOD, my good niggar!!!

And it also takes my mind too, F GM, for the people out of the loop, it stands for Female, Genital, Mutilation.

Well I think??? GOD and the devil, had a small talk??? How to give your touch (the devils touch!!!), to are sheep??? The devil was like, I know!!! I'll give them my touch, but the whole race will follow YOU!!!

Will I get sued, by a whole race now???

And I think???

They will be less sensitive emotionally, because we know, men are less sensitive, but losing your fine touch, will lead to your, mental emotions, going as well, because, all things are, connected in this life!!!

And most America also do that, to most of there boys, as well, and irony hits again!!!

Because America, also follows my good niggar!!!

Will this observation, change the whole world, or not???

Is it, an American culture, to sue a British charity??? It seem, like the whole world, has taken that to heart now!!! And my niggar, is sooooo disappointed, in American's, in helping out his twin, the devil, in this way.

In making easy money!!!

Meaning great life, but pain for eternity!!!

Also not being able to change, the direction of your thinking??? So bad things, run through your mind again and again!!!

But I have to go against that, and say, you win, but can you take that money/win, into the afterlife???

That win gives you, a guarantee place, into hell!!!

I also know, that America follow GOD, but do they know???

That they are also working, for the devil too??? By losing there virginity.

Like all the people, who have sued someone??? Had a, great life!!! But are in, great pain now!!! If gone from Earth now???

Then the, real devil children, will play with your soul, we know them, as imps, they'll say when, sticking you in pain!!! They'll say, "you wanted me/us???" "Now we paying you back, for entity!!!"

My 50/50 mind, say yes live like a king/queen, for 33 ish years???

Then pain, for eternity!!!

You can't die again, already dead, so pain, again and again, for eternity/forever!!!

I've kinda given you, a 50/50 choice???

The choice is yours to make???

Do you want to join, the devil, and his children??? For eternity???

Or help, my niggar out??? & a British charity, and the NHS now???

I'm kinda the key holder, in supporting the NHS, so

suing moi, is like suing everyone!!! In England, who use the NHS, do you, want too have, fun now??? Then see the devil, for entity???

It's why, we cannot, go to heaven/hell, there'll be no one left on Earth anymore, and hell would be empty!!!

I'm kinda working for, the devil now!!! In writing this book, But I'm giving you, the choice, too see him/not???

It's like for moi, playing a word game, the person who made it up, wants you to think??? In there terms of logic, yes that comes first, to moi, then illogical craziness, that may make you laugh at moi???

CHAPTER 22

....

This goes back too, the saying "never work, for your family!!!"

I didn't know, why at first???

Then it happened too someone, in my family!!!

Then I had too think why???

It came too me, it's the time frame, when you start or show up for work!!!

Real job, early, ready to work.

Family, show up, any time, to open the doors/shop???

Thank you, & good night again!!!

CHAPTER 23

In my life I don't, seem to go, the easy way round, because, that's not life, to moi, I needed to be, challenged, that to moi, is more interesting!!! Which also means, I have a gluttony for punishment, I don't have, an orgasms over the problem, just smile, when done, because I thought??? I'll not get that done???

I'll say it again, I listen to my elders, that's why, I'm broken now!!!

But life is kinda more interesting now, I know, you all think??? That's just, messed up!!! But that's just moi, messed up!!!

You always need too take a 50/50, look at life!!!

The good things, if done this way & bad things, if done, that way???

I kinda aim to be perfect, because now I've kinda become a perfectionist, when I'm cooking food, I know it's impossible, to reach!!! But still gives moi, a goal, to reach for!!! That's why I'm like, yeah yeah, and your option, please???

Was it, good/bad???

Do I live, or die??? 50/50 for you!!!

As I said, "there is no finishing line for moi!!!"

As I've been sent back, I kinda lost, mee wallet, well it slipped, out my coat pocket, on the bus ride into town, I walk, to make an appointment, to see, a G.P, when I was searching my coat, I couldn't find my wallet, so I went to the, bus company first, and reported it, then went to the police station to report it, if I left, my mobile phone number in it, to call moi if found, but NOTHING!!! Ah well a nice surprise, for them, when gone from here then???

If this was, still the old England, I think??? It would have been handed in??? I also did report it to the bus company, so someone might of handed it in, like the American saying goes, "you snooze, you lose!!!"

Another thing is, everything you touch, or keep???

You leave your essence, on the item, meaning it, still belongs too you!!!

Only then, can the thing/item be used by you!!!

The only way, too be free from the item is death!!! Or be given, to charity, not for personal gain!!!

I did just that, with just uni pound, for non Franchises out there??? It's one pound!!!

It went too Salisbury hospital, for there second MRI scanner!!!

Hey every little HELPS!!!

Then it belongs, to the universe!!! Unless someone else, holds on to it???

And they, didn't know???

It belongs to a broken person, or disabled person, as I'm still alive, that is classed as steeling, if not handed in!?!?!?

That also, goes for money, I was holding on too, due to the, memory value it has, and not the, face value of the print!!!

Why do, cats chase after mice???

When my niggar created them, he wanted too see them

fight, or chase each other, as it'll be more interesting, to see the outcome???

On the 7/11/16, my job coach said, "my findings, have no back up, to it/them"

As I'm a theory fool, like the book title, 50/50, I'm telling you, the out come, if done???

As Gregory House said, "everyone is stupid!!!" I know he is, a made up, charter on a TV show or a TV series!!!

But that also, includes moi, so everything, I've said, most of you will, probably do it/that??? Or not???

There's another thing I want too add, but can't say a word!!!

This would be, a new chapter!!!

Or include it, into the sleep section, that I done earlier???

Nah I'll just, hash it on the end of this 1, it's kinda, new info added to the sleep section, I talked about, I think???

Sleeping for 3 hours, your body gets cold, and looks to burning, your body fat, for energy to keep you warm, to be alive!!!

Then do simple maths, 3 is the starting point, then another 3 hours, more fat gets burnt off, they done the study, on sleep, but it was, 10 hours of sleep VS 5 hours of sleep, and the more sleep group won!!! So more sleep, gets you slim, I kinda came across, a more believe sleep time article, it was 8 hours VS 5 hours of sleep, and again, more sleep group won again!!!

Another way, you might get insomnia is too, re-sleep, but your, brain is all fixed up, and your ready to go, and do some, damage, on the world, or just go too work, if working???

As I said, the magic number, is 3!!! If you want too,

re-sleep??? 30 min's is max!!! If 33 min's, welcome to insomnia land/city, see 3 is the magic number!!! (you fool!!!)

So please, can you, only do 30 minutes X 2, once a day, when ever, you feel, like doing that???

It's the devil, who gave us, "big is better" well, he wanted, too see, how far, we'll go with that??? I'm a big idiot, or am I???

I've worked out, are sleeping times, they say 5-8 hours a night, for a normal person??? Sometimes, I get 4 and a bit, hours, I kinda know why!!!

This is my thinking??? I've worked out how or why, we sleep, the times we have/do???

It's the size, of your brain, big brain = less sleep the reason, came to my broken mind is.

1, Start off born, breathing your first breath, your first brain cells made!!!

2, Then seeing and smelling, then touching hot and cold, more brain cells, made or created!!!

3, A few years go by!!! A bit older, then learning to walk and talk.

More years go by.

4, Start Play school, more brain cells created.

5, Primary school, more brain cells created, like maths and better language skills, more brain cells created.

6, Secondary school, maybe another, language learnt, more brain cells created.

7, Maybe college, or work???

I'm a, curious cat, or willing too learn = even bigger brain, that's why 4 hours of sleep a night!!!

I think???

The same thing, applies too old people, willing to learn???

This knowledge comes from, my own family!!!

Take my dad, as an example, he seems to sleep 8 hours a night, he doesn't like to, learn new things!!! Like I said, learning = bigger brain, less sleep!!!

Now I think???

He stopped learning, in his late 20's???

And he can, only speak, Cantonese well!!!

He's been living in England, since 1969, he thinks he knows???

How to say "hello"

But if you, know Cantonese and English, in fact, he's saying prawn man, it just sounds similar to hello, just missing, the "o" sound, so he's har lo, meaning prawn man.

If I do, phonic sound.

In Cantonese, it's "har lo", prawn man, it just sounds similar.

Even tho, I've got a broken brain, I can speak, English well, chav English, like "what's up brov???"

I can count 1-??? In English, I don't know where you, want moi too stop???

1-??? In Cantonese, not quite too sure on the, 1000+ area???

1-12 in French, and maybe, 20 area, don't know why??? I'm still holding on too that information/knowledge???

CHAPTER 24

....

The old England, is dead now!!!

This was, taken off, Facebook, on the 27/5/16.

R.I.P. United Kingdom!!! You went soft on discipline. You raised the cost of living so high that both parents are always at work, rather than spending time with their children. You took God out of schools. Parents were told 'No you can't discipline your kids'. Kids had rights blah, blah, blah. Well. U.K!!! You shall reap what you sow, and we have lost a whole generation and turned them into selfish, disrespectful brats who have no respect for people, property or authority! Things need to change! Copy & paste if you have the guts to!!!"

I've had the guts to share have you!!!

This is, so true!!!

I might get, my ass sued into next week, or beyond that???

But it feels like, we all are following, the foot steps of America, all I seem to care about is moi!!! From my point of view is, old America was good, like the 60's, up until the millennium???

It feels like, the whole now seems, to be following, there foot steps???

Like when, I, got off the bus, that day, a normal person, got off, then people, waiting for the bus people, thought all good, too go and get on, and I was still waiting to get off!!!

So I allowed them, all to get on, then the bus driver closed the door, then drove, for a bit, then I had to speak up!!! Then he reopened, the doors, and I still said, to the bus driver, "good bye, have a good day". Why am I, slow??? After my crash, my balance is still a bit, poo!!! Like being in, a moving object, e.g. Bus, it takes more energy and concentration, to move, or balance myself well!

The old England, was polite to others, not just thinking of them self, it seems to me, we are following, the foot steps of America.

Are we???

Following the, foot steps of America???

Working for the devil???

By suing everyone, so we have a, great life now!!! Followed by pain, for eternity???

So I have to be, kinda safe!!! But that's kinda boring to moi, like when, I have a normal bus ride, the older generation, are polite to the bus driver, too say "good bye" the younger generation, or new style, of living, just walk off the bus, no thank you or anything!!!

I met an author on the 9/6/16 she said, "you have to be, careful, with the American public now!!!" Because they all work for the devil now!!! Without knowing it!!!

Like I'm working for him, now!!! Too, if I get sued!!! By anyone???

I'm sending, those people down to him, and I'll have to go, on BBC world news, to tell the whole world, these are the evil people on earth now!!! Suing a British charity, I have to leave, the choice, up to the individual, on what to do, do you, sue moi/not??

So great life now, or short time Spence, followed by

pain, forever??? Or you'll be, raving it up 24/7, no rest, for you when dead???

There is a video I've seen, he says "short time gain, followed by, long term pain!!!"

How true, is that for moi.

I was told to do it.

CHAPTER 25

....

This chapter is dedicated too, all non believers out there!!!

I know, you only believe, in the physical side of things, like you can, grab hold of, and shake the shit out of, and hold on to things, for non believers???

You don't have to read on NOW???

If your still here???

Alright, lets just say, you are GOD, in a wide open space, then created suns, with a gravitational pull, then placed planets in there, still a bit BORING!!!

Then thought???

Creatures are needed, to entrain, me a bit more, like I said, dinosaurs, are a bit boring, eat, shit and sleep, then decided, humans are needed, to find and discover new things down here!!!

O yeah I need to say, I'm out there, then Jesus, he came to us, then later on books came along, needed to document everything, up to this point, then create writers, to put everything down, in books, so the knowledge can live on!!!

CHAPTER 26

My broken mind has worked out, the beginning of the afterlife, heaven will be, the good choices, you made in life, with that story, continuing on in heaven???

It'll be like entering a, sort of physical cinema, the movie is, your life on earth!!!

It'll show you, why, you've gone to heaven/hell, but you'll say, when watching it???

Sorry I can't, give the game away!!!

CHAPTER 27

After watching "The Truman show" that's GODS, day everyday, just replace, Truman with your name, you are the main charter, it does, depend if he has, flicked over too your channel, which is your life???

That's why, I'm back to drive again, but only out of my town!!!

When out of my town, I can let my hair loose, my former passengers, will say "crazy man!!!" But I like too, push the boundaries of life, a 50/50 thing for you!!! Will I, crash/not???

Research goes, you are more likely, to crash in your own town or a well known road.

That's why, I let my hair loose, when out of my town. (how can I let my hair loose, if it's short???)

But what happened to moi??? I've become, a number!!!

A rappers mind, seems quite like mine???

Being able too, pull random words, out of thin air!!!

CHAPTER 28

This kinda, goes out to, Stephen Fry, GOD has made the perfect reality, but it sooo boring too watch!!!

A scene was written in, The Matrix, where the robots did make a perfect world, but they lost, thousands of crop, aka people, to be there generators, we need happiness and sadness, to feel alive!!!

Like my book title 50/50.

See now I given you, the choice, to sue my ass, and the whole of England, or just, let it go???

THE END AGAIN!!!

Have an, awesome life, my readers??? Fool time, over and out!!!

CHAPTER XXX

O no!!!

A XxX, CHAPTER!!!

I'm just, messing with your, imagination here!!!

Where will you go???

Will you go???

O no I'm steering you, to naked villi, or will you go to the, blood and guts root???

See another 50/50 thing for you!!!

It's your life, so it's your imagination???

CHAPTER XXX-2

....

O no a squeal!!!

Nah!!!

Just messing with your, imagination!!! Again!!!

More random junk, came to my busted mind!!!

Why do the, "good, die, young???"

Well this, kinda happened, in my life, my version is???

Sharing the love!!!

Meaning do you use, your time, too look after, someone else???

There was someone I knew, but never met!!!

He did die, at age of 58 years old, I think???

He owned a restaurant, he was the boss, but looked after all his customers!!!

I think???

He died, serving his customers???

The problem is now, is everyone has, selfish love!!!

Only taking care, of them self!!!

May we meet???

Another 50/50, for you, sorry to ask you too, spend money, too meet moi!!! I'm a broken bum now!!! Even tho, I've got half of your money now, I think??? You'll want too???

CHAPTER ???

··

This chapter, kinda goes out too, Yan, can't quite remember or spell, his surname, I think it goes??? Yan Libodyhil???

He was travelling to, New Zealand, with a stop over, in Hong Kong, then connecting to, New Zealand.

Now he's a smart traveller, he learnt or picked up English, from "The fresh prince of Bel air" and he knows a bit of French as well!!! He's a Belorussia n, from Belarus.

We met on the 2/11/16, as I was travelling to, Hong Kong, for more treatment, that's why I want, England to use, longer needles in acupuncture, and bring the cure, too dementia, as a bonus, for using longer needles. And I'm sorry to Yan, I didn't ask you, if I could, use your name??? Even tho, my busted brain, was planning it out!!!

And I, also told him the title, of this book 50/50, will he buy this book???

And tell moi, how was his trip, was???

HOW???

Now time for, chicken!!! Do I hear??? Mark Oakley, saying chicken boy???

Eat well that's why, we are here!!! And no more war, going on now!!!

On the 11/12/16, I had a life like dream???

I just got out, of bed, went to load up my PC, too connect my Fitbit watch, so I can see, how much time I had sleeping???

It was kinda strange???

My PC desktop, reloaded it self, meaning all the icon on it, have moved or completely disappeared???

Then a few hours, later after a nap, I reloaded up, my PC, and everything is back too, how I left it, the previous night???

I also worked out, WHY I'm still eating chicken now!!!

CHAPTER ???-2

....

Going back too, the last Chapter, I've also, worked out WHY I'm still here!!!

I use too live, by this saying, "it's do, or die!!!"

I did die!!!

So, my good niggar, put moi back down here!!! And my evil niggar, he knew, I'll do hidden evilness for him???

I can't say anything, because the evilness, has been done!!! And it can only go one way!!! Even my broken mind, can't find an escape???

That's why, I keep on moving!!! Or doing things!!! I just don't like too, stop!!!

Because boredom, settles in quick in my brain/mind!!!

And also enjoyment is gone, quickly as well, ooo fun, gone next please???

No!!!

It wasn't a dream!!!

Because I've just checked, my Fitbit log, and it says, I've had 4 hours of sleep!!!

But I don't know why, my computer desktop has returned, back to how I left it, the previous night???

CHAPTER 33

....

<u>I think???</u>

I'm trying UT out now, which is urine therapy, it's not quite 50/50, if there are videos, on YouTube, with people saying there benefits from there own urine.

I look at it as, being pure irony, again!!!

We are our own healers!!!

Yes science, is there to help us all out, but UT, is personalised, just to your own body!!! As it comes from you!!!

I can say it works best, on your, own skin, because I had a foot cul lass on my broken leg!!!

Due to moi, putting all my body weight, on that one spot!!!

I've kinda, been doing UT(urine therapy), for 3 days, OOO no, make that 5 days, and my, cul lass, skin has gone back to normal skin now!!! And the, ironic thing is, my GP said there is. nothing I can rub, into it now, I have too see, a foot specialist, to cut it off!!! Just because the main part has gone!!! Don't give up, until it has gone, completely!!! Because my skin, is still dry, but normal, meaning it's still infected, just be a stubborn fool, just try to reach, for perfection, I know it's impossible, but gives you something, to reach for!!!

You're giving your skin, double trouble, by drinking your urine, and rubbing it, into your skin, then you'll heal faster from it.

I'm kinda like, what the hell!?!?!?

Your own, urine works a treat!!!

And I didn't have to go ask for help!!!

All I can say is, just man up to it!!!

Science says, it's 95 %, made of water, just let a little go, then catch the rest.

Like I said, it's your life!!!

So you can, do it or not???

I have done it, and it worked for moi!!!

But another way, you might look at is, I'm broken person, so it'll work for me!!!

But there are people, on YouTube, who made videos, showing or telling you, it works!!!

Another famous person, you all know, Madge AKA Madonna, she said, pee on your own foot, to get rid of athletes foot, while in the shower, my own take, on it is, in the morning, pee into a cup/mug??? Dip your finger in it, rub the area, that needs healing??? Let it soak in, and do the rest of your morning clean??? When washing your face, use the towel or flannel, to wipe your feet clean, or the area with, your urine on it??? O no!!! I've just reread that, rub your feet at night, and let your, pee heal you over night, then wipe your feet clean in the mooning.

After watching, I robot, the difference in us, and robots, is we can, just make STUPID DECISIONS, robots, have to follow logic, because it's there best decision for us, or in that situation, right there and then???

O yeah, deep sleep/rem sleep, helped my broken brain, because fatigue, when I was awake, didn't seem that bad, like 3 again, anything over 3 hours of deep sleep is good, for my busted brain!!! Because that's what deep sleep can do, for your brain, fix itself well!!!

Good bye, and good night, or good morning, to all my readers???

From this book.

CHAPTER 34

O no!!!

More random knowledge, about the brain, well I think???

If your faced, with a, challenge in life!!!

I think???

That knowledge, stays with you!

From my experience is, still have my Honda knowledge, but no memory, of being an office boy, or to be, political correct, admin or an administrator!

See my thinking goes???

Honda mechanic new knowledge, meaning new brain cells, made in the brain! Office boy then, that job was too, easy to pour moi!(for me!) So no new, brain cells created, in my brain.

I think???

That was 2004 period???

I was told.

Jobless for a year???

Then admin assistance, for a year, I think???

Now new life!!!

With most of my, old memories???

As I died, it now goes back, to the day, I was born, then jump to the 27/8/1986, when me and my dad, went to look at a shop space, before it was turned, into the Chef Peking, also moving from

Cirencester to Salisbury, and living above the restaurant, before we moved to Harnham, in 1987 in Salisbury!!!

CHAPTER 35

··

Ahhh, I am, the book title!!!

As my broken mind is, still trapped in the, late 90's.

As of today!!!

The 11/04/17, I got shown, society has changed, everything you say, is 100% true!!!

Now I really feel like, a cave man! Eating food, with bones in it clean!

Like back in 1995, we were throwing bad words around, like a big ass joke**!!!**

Not so now, due to the millennium, coming round!

What I've done now, is called a self rape!!!

But I hear you, asking how???

As it takes 2, to tango, back to the point!!!

It takes 2 people, to commit rape!!!

To be PC(Politically Correct), I've f***** myself up the ass!!!

Now I leave you, with a wrong, mental image of myself, being raped!!! By moi!!!

CHAPTER 36

··

If something happens, in my life, sorry to say!!!

No copy cats!!!

I'm the original monkey!!!

I started it, and wrote this book about it, so maybe???

3 centres or maybe more, down the line???

Or maybe not???

Another 3 millenniums, down the line???

O NO, Old Sarum houses!!! Now it's 462 houses.

On the 31st of January 2018, they are having another meeting, more info, has come to my broken mind!!!

If houses built???

It'll be the, physical gate way, into HELL!!!

First off the company, will go to HELL, if new or old workers start in that company??? All construction workers, who built the houses, then a HUGH KICK IN THE NUTS!!!

Any new families, who move into them, new houses???

SORRY TO CALL, THE FORMER OFFICERS, MEN/WOMAN DOGS.

As a saying comes to my broken mind, I guesstimate???

You've heard it???

"It's let sleeping dogs, LIE!!!"

That means!!! Do not do anything, to the former, world war 1 airfield, I know, the devils offering you lots of money, to build houses, on the airfield, to house more people, on there!!!

If done, the former officers, will wake up, to give you pain, when dead!!!

CHAPTER 37

....

This chapter, kinda goes out to, Chester Bennigton, O no!!!

I'm doing an assumption??? You know the saying??? An assumption, is the mother of all f-ups!!!

Well he has, graced the news, a lot because, he died on the 20th of July in 2017, he did say, in/on a, YouTube video, life doesn't give you, a postcard, when your rich and famous, saying life will be easier now!!!

And how, true is THAT???

I'm a fan of Linkin Park, but not a hardcore fan!!! It's because, I've not got, some of their albums!!!

Like 1 of them, is called "a tribute to Linkin Park", so that's not there work!!! No Chester screaming away, Just used their name!!! If I had, the money to throw away??? I'll be like, it's in, my bag son!!!

Sorry to say!!! It feels like, fate has stepped in here!!! I know, that's a poor excuse, to put my blame, on the unknown!!! But it feels like, he's suppose to help, a British charity, I know he's American, and I've never met him, in this physical realm/life!!! But I think??? He'll be happy to, as he'll live on, in more memories, to the other people, who will purchase this book??? And maybe listen, to his screaming??? It's all good, in my broken view of things, just my option, on their music, and the band has, also supported different charities in this world, as well.

On to another Welsh band, the lead singer said, "leave

your mark, in life!!!" I'm not asking you, to be famous and kill yourself and sleep with kiddies, Just leave an, impression on people's mind!!!

This might come across, as a downer, to all people, thinking of self suicide, PLEASE DON'T!!!

If done??? You'll think??? Pain is over!!!

O really, as you enter into hell, where pain, is on 24/7, to forever, to no end!!! But Chester has a slight loop hole, I think??? As he has, given joy to so many people on Earth, so maybe he can do a trade, with the devil??? And that's why, you need to make/leave your mark in life.

CHAPTER 38

Life's just a big joke to moi!!!

It wants you to, trade your time for money, and the kick in the nuts is, the devil will be waiting for you??? When your time is up, so what do you do???

Make good memories, the devil, will play you bad/poor images to you, but be like, it's only just a movie, I'm dead now, from the physical realm now!!! So that shit, doesn't bothers moi anymore!!! I know, it'll be hard, not to look, and have no eye lids to close, just play your memories, of the good times??? Turned around.

CHAPTER 39

Thank you YouTube, there is a video on there, talking about old souls. My thinking goes, back too!!!

Summer of 1996, when I/we, my family had just moved into Ford!!!

The house we, moved into, cost a well how to say??? Back in 1995, when house prices were low!!! The 5 bed room we moved into, cost £148,000, well just a little more, well I'm not, that STUPID, to say the real price!!! Even tho, I still remember it, after 20+ years now!!! See my busted brain holds on to useless junk!!! That was back in 1995, what can that, get you now??? A 3 bed if LUCKY!!! We came into, that large amount of money, after my dad sold, our other restaurant, in Romsey or near Romsey, the area was called North Baddesley.

I was only, 14 years old, that's when, the rich, life gambler, came out to play.

It was like, I don't really care, about money then, now it's like, I only need enough, to fill my fat belly!!! And live comfortably, and another old souls video, says old souls, don't care about materialist things, aka money!!!

Another slight thing, it's the devil, who hiked up the prices, of everything!!! He just wants your soul!!! Ah but you Blam inflation, that's the devils, physical hand in this physical realm, as he can't come to this realm, to do it!!!

Something else came to my broken mind, money, doesn't matter to old souls, because, they lived once and died, and they couldn't take the money with them!!! So money, doesn't matter, that much too them.

New or young souls, just want money, to make there life easier/better!!!

But it only matters, in this physical realm, as an old Chinese saying goes, person goes to heaven!!! Money stays in the bank!!! And that will happen too!!! Another thing came to my mind, it's the 18 year old limit!!!

Meaning, when you die, at 18 or not???

I think???

That's where the life judging begins, if greedy before 18, doesn't really matter, if greedy, 18 or after, then that, looks like an, afterlife rave 24/7, no time to sleep or rest!!!

And also, I think??? Taking 3 naps, is the tops if your broken or not, it's down to your body/brain, remembering, to take, 15 mins off your sleep time, when you do bed, at the end of the day.

It's simple maths, 15 mins + another 15mins = 30 mins, and add another 15 to that, and you get 45 mins off your long sleep time, that's why 3 is max!!! Because you don't, I don't want you too lose, an hour off your sleep time!!!

Hey I've done it!!!

Just giving you another 50/50 choice, like I said it's your life???

And I'll take the harder way in life!!!

It was too see, if I lived, or not???

It sure does, make life more interesting, to live that way then!!! I only noticed that, as I'm alive again now!!! And a poker star, said that too!!!

And then I moved it on, too my driving my car, when I was 18, it was like, will I crash or not???

Like I said, my former passengers, though my driving was, crazy!!!

But if crazy, I'll be a penniless, broken fool now!!!

It's just, pure irony again!!!

They say, you are most likely to crash on, well known roads, that's why, I drove like an ass-hole, out of my town!!! (still signalling on round a bouts, like a learner!!!)

And the other thing is, too see, if others failed, in front of moi(me)

So I would be like, you can go first then???

Then in 1998, I think the, second old soul, came out to play???

That soul, I think is or was, a chef???

That's when I thought of, steam hamburgers, and meat dumplings, it's good because the oil released from the burgers, get soaked up by the meat dumplings pastry skin, so you have, meat flavoured pastry, and add vinegar to the meat dumplings as well.

The third soul is, I think??? Is a private, in the British army??? So he was on the front line in World War 1, it kinda goes down too the fact!!! That they wanted to, build 470 houses on the air field in Ford, and that air field dates back to the World War 1!!! Meaning I had to, stand up for it, it's too show my/our respect, for the officers, in that war, if houses built??? My thinking goes, "quick gain!!! E.g. Houses built, meaning money made!!! Then long term pain, but I have to change that too, eternal pain."

Because hell, is your new destination now!!!

On the 31st of January 2018, they are having another meeting, more info, has come to my broken mind!!!

If houses built???

It'll be the, physical gate way, into HELL!!!

First off the company, will go to HELL, if new or old workers start in that company??? All construction workers, who built the houses, then a HUGH KICK IN THE NUTS!!!

Any new families, who move into them new houses???

Hey the devil will take anything that goes!!!

They've decided now, to build offices on there, ah well, it'll still be, the road to HELL!!!

The forth soul is, a writer, from the 12th or the 16th century, I had some memories from 1626th I think??? Well I had some flash backs, as he used, candle light to do his writing, well come to think about it, he came out during 1998, when I got a laptop, from HK (Hong Kong), that's when I started doing a, diary, I call it, The Book of Randomness!!! I think??? It's Somewhere in my junk room now??? I've written 2 books, and I've got a, good grasp of English, I think??? And my own knowledge of simple Fransiour aka French as well, and I'm doing, phonetic Cantonese, into English, as well, like the start of this book!!!

So I don't know???

If your a curious cat??? To buy the other 2 books??? To help out a, British charity???

Another extreme thing, that has happened to moi, after a brain injury is, I can get drunk now, on alcohol, but I, still don't reach for the bottle!!!

That's kinda extreme, have a car crash, just too get drunk!!!

Because if I did, my healed brain, would be a waste of time and money!!!

Like I said, it'll give moi, dementia again, if I drank it!!!

CHAPTER 40

∙∙∙

I just wanted to, add more knowledge to it, being a psychologist, they should know, words don't mean, I say "shit!!!" It should be, anything!!! And action, speak louder then words, you have to deal with bad apples, here and there, in your life!!! Because, you chose to help out, messed up people!!! And you've got the money, to help others, so you have to deal with bad people, it's your job, because, you received a nice lump of money/cash, to do that job!!! Well now I've been told, that the girl I offended, has gone/ left, so you won't see, a blond psychologist or robber, I say, in or down at Totton brain injury group UK, anymore now!!! A worker/care there, though it was good, to have a well trained psychologist there!!! As she did it, for her day time job, well I kinda proved her wrong, as she's not a well trained psychologist, just a robber with the title, in front of her Nome, I should say name!!!

And on YouTube, they say that, "introvert people have", psychologist traits as well, I kinda was, or still am, an introvert, with a slice of, out going randomness, and they also said, "old souls, don't care about, material goods", so I kinda, a broken psychologist, without the training, but the life experience, so am I???

I think??? It's because, they've lived once!!! And money only matters in this psychical realm, meaning I'll rather see the money help the world!!! To make it a better place, that's why this book is called 50 50, me 50%, the other half goes to, the charities, I'm apart of now!!!

She won't most likely come across, any bad apples in her job!

It's because, they can't afford, her time!!!

It was nice of her, to give her time up, to brain injury group UK, then enter, the broken bum!!! Moi!!!

This came too, my broken mind!!!

It's like, real psychologist, vs trained psychologist, meaning I've, had the life experience, vs book knowledge.

I word raped her!!!

My criminal psychologist mind, comes out to play, o no!!!

I've kinda of, given rapist, a slight loop hole, in my busted, view on the law!!! To moi, a rape, is an unplanned event, like wham, balm, thank you mam!!! As I've told her, that'll she will be raped!!! It can't be rape!!! Because I've, wrote it's down, in plain black and white writing. It'll just be, plain sexual abuse!!! Just my view, on my situation!!!

I've given myself, another 50 50 thing???

nah, the law will be hard, on my busted ass!!!

CHAPTER 41

It's my use of language, that goes back too, 1995, when that robber was born!!! So she didn't spread the love back then, as that saying came from America.

But it was, attached to another word, the word or phrase was, "love rape", because we were spreading the "love" back in 1995, everyone was spreading the love, if you remember back too then??? Meaning we were hugging people, still fully clothed, at my school, we added, the word "rape" which is an unplanned and unintentional hug.

Meaning her mind, lead to a real rape, WHY, would I do that???

I know, it's WRONG!!! O yeah, it's your thinking???

Wanting to please myself, using your body, to please moi, why would I, do that???

If done??? I'll be like, ooo pleasure, then gone, next please!!!

If I had done a, real life rape, why would GOD, send moi back to Earth???

Is it too, rape you??? Because your a blond physiologist, helping broken people and as your blond, nah I can't say it!!!

Because if typed??? ALL BLONDS WILL HATE MOI!!!

It's too, mind rape you!!! Too see if you, used your time well, to have that title, in front of your nome(name)???

I think???

It's to sort out, the good, from the bad, as I work for them both now!!!

It'll be expected from a, criminal physiologist, but come on life isn't, an easy ride!!!

Because if you do a, well paid job, STRESS, has too go, hand in hand, with the job or money, that comes your way!!!

CHAPTER 42

....

Another little bit of help???

If you have a corn on your foot???

Probably not???

If on the, big toe or another part of the foot???, can you, put Vapour rub on it first, then seal it in with Vaseline, before you go to bed, put vapour on your corn first, then seal in, with the Vaseline, if on the side of the big toe, can you wrap up, with tissue paper or kitchen roll??? Snip off a piece of kitchen roll, or tear it off, I score it with a knife, to be ripped cleanly off, then wrap up your big toe, put a sock on to hold it in place, so the liquid, doesn't get soaked up by the sock, when woken up, the next morning??? Can you please, remove your socks, it's to let your feet breath!!! AH NO, another 50 50 choice, for you??? You can, also remove the, kitchen roll or tissue paper??? When your sock has been removed.

Or you can put the sock back on, then bed again??? Hey it's your life, so can you CHOOSE PLEASE???

I say, or use kitchen roll, because tissue will break up or get worn down, and it'll, stay in you sock, then it'll get taken into, the washing machine, which will lead to, clogging up your washing machine. .

Well my corn, has kinda gone, after 8 months, I think???

That's another 50 50, for tu(you), will it be quicker/longer??? Pour tu(for you???)

I have to, due to not, walking like, a ladies man anymore!!!

But a person with a brain injury now!!!

So kinda messed up!!! Sideways style!!!

More YouTube videos, about apple skin/peels, they are good for you, due to them having, good chemicals in them which your body needs, they didn't say, it will also help you drop 1 large, if you had an apple, a day??? But it may take, 24 hours??? Or quicker, like 12 hours??? To drop the apple out, with the food you ate during your day?? If a lot of apples are eaten??? And they say, one apple a day, I say 2 apples a day??? The max is 3 or three apples, One in the morning for breakfast, then another one, for lunch or dinner??? It's your life, so you can choice please??? Another 50 50 for you???

CHAPTER 43

Life has the last laugh!!!

It will laugh at you, when you are dead, because, you didn't open your mind, to try out, other types of food or drink!!! And doing, quick gains, which will bring you, long term pain or eternal pain, so can you please!!! Take your time???

Mainly food, not alcohol, because that's the devils blood!!! I talked about alcohol, Life to moi is, eating, or having a different mouth experience, like I didn't know, the Italians, where on to the experience already, you get, from food, like have a bread stick to start things off, you get a crunchy feeling too start with, then have a bite of pizza or a mouth full of spaghetti/pasta, you get a soft feeling, in your mouth full of food, when swallowed, have another bread stick again, to get the feeling of crunchiness back in your mouth, and then back to, pizza or pasta???

After watching, "The day the Earth stood still", there was a line in it said, "no one ever dies!!!" that is, kinda true, just your physical body dies, or is worn out, then your soul, or sprit is freed from this, physical realm, or body!!!

Something I read that came up, animals, don't feel pain!!! They do feel pain!!! That's how, they learn, to stay away from, FIRE!!!

If they didn't???

We'll have a lot more, chicken and steak burgers!!! With intestine, to go with it!!! Mmm how yummy is that???

CHAPTER 44

....

Another YouTube video.

Warming up cars, on the YouTube video, the person said, you can just start your car up, and go, due to most cars being, fuel injected now!!! And the car engine sitting in less, viscous oil, meaning it's less dense oil, that the engine has to move in, if you, don't know that word??? Or have no science knowledge???

And he didn't say, that you'll increase your mpg, if done??? That way is a way, to increase your engine in drinking fuel like that???

It was when car engines, that had carburettor in them, you had to, fully warm up the engine!!! For the engine to run/perform well

A good example, I thought of is, honey the liquid, or the solid version, now if cold water is added??? The honey will not, de-solve into the water, if boiled water added, just give the boiled water a little time, too melt the honey, hey the hot water, is too hot, for the honey, meaning it'll kill off the goodness found in the honey!!! Then the honey will mix into the water, similar thing with a warm car engine, in which will = easer moving car engine parts!!! Which means, less fuel used which again = more money, in your pocket!!!

I'm back to give you, more help, on random things??? I'm helping you on how to drink warm honey water, please do not use, just boiled kettle, water in honey!!! It's because, the temperature of, hot water, kills off, the goodness found in honey, so I use, 150 ml, of cold boiled water, as it has, no more lime scale in it, if you live in the south of England??? Or have chalk pits, in your area??? Then add, just boiled water to the mix, make it up too 250 ml of water, or 1 cup of water, of the 8 cups, that you need everyday??? And they said that, honey water, on an empty stomach, in the morning, helps you to improve your eye sight, well, I'm doing that now, they didn't say how long it'll take??? So it's a wip, not a leather whip!!! You dirty minded people out there??? But a Work, In, Progress, WIP, so I, don't know when, it'll be the end??? And another thing, I'm trying out is, eat raw garlic, to improve you eye sight, because it contains, chemicals too help out, if you suffer from heart disorders??? Help remove cancer cells!!! Help you out, if you have, high blood pressure??? Helps you if you've got a cold??? Male and females, if you suffer from, hair loss, drinking warm water, will bring your hair back!!! I know because, after secondary school and college, I gelled my hair, to look stylish, gel kinda pulls out your hair gently, so I kind, thinned out on top, but after doing a water breakfast, my hair has come back!!! It'll help you out, if you suffer from Alzheimer or Dementia??? And 1 last thing is, Diabetes!!!

Bhp you'll never use it, or reach it, due to the, output of it, is so high up, in the rev range, on petrol cars??? And in England, we don't have, long enough, straight roads, for it to be done???

O NO, a plug for, turbo diesel cars, they have an early, torque output, but dies, if revved pass, the torque output range or the turbo output point???

CHAPTER 45

It's time vs money, do you, waste time, to save money???

Or use time, and lose money???

As there is, a saying out there, "EVERY LITTLE PENNY, HELPS"

I know it's small, and you feel, like you wasted, a good amount of time!!!

Or do you, break down, and dance while warming up your car engine??? Another YouTube video, they say, no need to warm up car engines, but another video, demonstrated how long, it should take, to warm up a car, the video showed, it took 00:07:48, but you have too take a pinch of salt, but I say 3 tonnes, well not that much!!! Unless you want diabetes type 1??? I didn't know, salt acts the same as sugar, in it needing insulin to dilute it, or make it, normal for your body, I mean it took, a carburettor engine 33 mins to warm up, to run well, I think??? It was around about, the 30 min mark, that's why I said 33. That'll be the same for, the first generation, of fuel injected cars, from 1985-1999, then time moves on, and so does technology, so now it's more like a minute – 3 minutes, as they say, the magic number is 3???

Every bit of movement, is good for your body, OK, not break dancing, just do stretching for your body then, for it to move, more freely, so you can, move more easily, everyday.

Another video, on about reheating breast milk, if refrigerated???

PLEASE, can you not, nuke it!!! Aka, microwave it!!! Or maybe, on a, low heat heat???

Like 300 watt, I know that's low!!! But every, little helps!!! But radiation, has touched the milk, so it maybe off??? I don't know, because I've not done, any research into it??? Then heat it up, using water in a sauce pan???

Get the milk warm up to, body temperature, use boiled kettle water, then heat it up using the fire on your stove, kind of shortcut for you to heat up the milk sat in the water??? With the leftover boiled water, you can make a drink, for yourself, coffee/tea it's your choice, in the poison you choose, aka drink, as it's your drink???

I know, this is more work, for you!!!

But you are, feeding your future child, will he/she, return the favour to you, when they've grown up??? Or look after you, when you are old???

Can you please do so???

But it's your life???

CHAPTER 46

··

Now turn over, and Zzz Zzz Zzz!!! Aka sleep!!!

Did yee, or still reading on???

DAM I'VE TURNED YOU, INTO A CURIOUS CAT!!!

Kinda another YouTube video, well, it works for moi, it's you need too, make white noise in your head, and it'll send you off to sleep, well, what is the, white noise???

Well I just go mmmmmmmmmmmmmm, or ah ah ah, but held longer or repeated, over and over again??? It's your life, so you can choose please??? I do that a few times, then, my mind just switches off, well, it's good for over active minds, like mine, that's why, some people, get 4 hours of sleep a night, like one time, I had 4:28 of sleep, because my busted mind fixed, it self quickly and others can also out there??? Because they can, fix there mind quicker, due to the, over activeness.

I don't clock watch, how then do I/you know, my sleep time??? Clock watching, gives you stress, like, I got to be up in XX:XX, and that stress you out, while trying too fall asleep, it's the Mi watch I wear, I had 1:06 mins of deep sleep, 4:20 of light sleep, but under my 3 hours of deep sleep needed, every single night, too feel dam good the next day???

WHY QUESTION MARKS???

Well 1 time, I had or got, 4:18 of deep sleep, and still felt rough!!!

That's the problem with a brain injury!!! Feeling rough, most day, well just moi!!!

If night time NOW??? Bon nuit, or Good night.

If not go out, and try new foods then???

I'm back, to help you???

Or to cause you, more trouble???

CHAPTER 47

∙∙

Something I've kinda noticed, with life or in life, you have to put in the time, for it to return, back to you, well!!!

The only thing I've noticed is, in the food industry, you have to, put in the time, for it to return to you, later on in the day, my observation is, this man started, frying stuff to be sold, when he opens the shop or restaurant, he started at 9:00 am, but he's not open until 11:00 am, so he was preparing stock, 2 hours before he opened, then I arrived at 15:30 pm, and his shop was hip and happening, not dancing, or moving down the road/street, well it was just busy, with 20+ heads, in the restaurant eating, compared to another person I knew, he just opened the shop, waiting for people to arrive, he was busy first, when his shop was new in town, but we all know, new things, fade fast!!!

CHAPTER 48

Another thing came too my mind!!!

There is a, saying out there, "scared body, = good life, pristine body, is a so so life"

I'm not telling you, to scare up your body!!!

Just take a walk, on the wilder side of life,

Some of my scares, are medical scares, to keep moi alive!!!

And some scares are, due to moi, being a clum-sie fool!!!

As every scare, has a story behind it, will it be, a good story or poor story???

But due to moi, walking too my destiny, it has scared up, my body up!!!

I'm back because, as a new friend said, "I treat life, like a, buffet", trying all types of food, will you too???

Good or bad, 50/50 for you!!!

If you think???

That's bad tasting food, it might just be good too moi???

CHAPTER 49

· ·

This has come to my mind, as I'm a curious cat, I watched another YouTube video, it was on about, lack of vitamin B12, it kinda has, the same or similar problems, as having a head injury.

I've NOT ASKED, my GP, to pill me up yet???

So it's a WIP???(work, in, progress???)

He'll rather play it safe, by nicking my blood, to see if it is, lacking of vitamin B12???

CHAPTER 50

....

This saying came to my broken mind, it's "money verses time", well it's the devil asking you, do you want too, see him or not???

I think??? That saying came out, in the late 1990, or was it??? Millennium time???

And to be his new buddy, for entirety, it's which matters, too you more???

Is it money???

If that's your answer, it became the bad choice, when 1940, came round, due to the sins coming into play then!!!

I know, you'll all be, asking how do I know that date???

My GOOD NIGGAR, he kinda, came down with moi, when we met, but gone now!!!

Because I think???

I've become a, safe and boring mofo, with no car to drive!!! And my brother said, or claims, I have no more meads, running around my broken body, and I was a bit too inquisitive, as well, if you had someone, sitting on your shoulder, seeing a possible future or outcome, why wouldn't you ask him??? You all thinking??? WHY NOT WIN THE LOTTERY???

If won, will I donated, the money, too charity!!!

And another reason, came too my, broken mind!!! The sins, are a well, HIDDEN EVIL!!! You think??? That you, haven't been evil, it's just the sins, are well hidden!!! You think??? All good!!! Haven't been, proper evil, e.g. Killing people, but the sins, are evil, like you, ONLY LOOKING, OUT FOR, YOURSELF!!!

CHAPTER 51

As they say, "life's a lesson," which means, to moi, you are the student, it doesn't matter, how old you are, everyday in life is, class time, you only learn, the little things in life now, if schools finished or has it??? Like now in 2018, social media, has become a big thing, do you become a student, and learn how things run, or be an old person, set in there ways, and watch time pass you by???

You have to, KEEP AN, OPEN MIND!!!

Is it Wright or wrong??? Still a lesson, in my busted view, on things, will you choose, the good or bad choice??? In your life/situation???

CHAPTER 52

··

This is new info, to moi, please can you, not eat food, then brush your teeth!!! It's due to, your saliva, still being in food burning mode!!! I know, I said wait an hour, or the interweb says "30 minutes for your saliva to go back too normal???" But as you're awake, it'll stay close, to that mode, all day!!! It only goes away, when you go too bed!!! Because that's when your body resets it's self!!! Tooth paste, is what it, says on the tin!!! Paste, meaning you'll be pasting, food burning saliva, on to your teeth, which will erode away the enamel, found on your teeth!!! In which will give you sensitive teeth.

So my suggestion is, which I do, and I only see the dentist, once a year!!!

I know, they say, "see the dentist, twice a year!!!" But if the dentist, tells you, only once a year!!! It's coming from a, professional point of view!!!

Well I read, another saying, came from America, "It's why, doesn't GOD, kill the DEVIL???"

As I'm here still, I can tell you why!!!

They are twins!!!

So how can he, kill his brother??? If someone was evil, in your family??? Do you have the heart too, knock them off???

That's where the saying comes from if twins had??? 1 good person, aka god, and 1 evil person, aka the devil, the universe is the dad, he made everything!!! And made his sons, to entertain him!!! Same goes for, them both!!!

(HAPTER 53

Myths or are they, not working on my busted brain??? Maybe another, 50/50 pour tu???

Well the first myth is, sleeping again!!! They say, you should get, more deep sleep again, because you've, just come out of light sleep, that's bs, too moi!!!

But I read it, on the, Interweb some where???

That it's a myth, and they didn't say why???

My busted thinking goes??? Brain all fixed up, time to get up and rip the world, a new 1, or just do, your normal daily things??? Or in my world, cause more trouble, to people that know moi???

CHAPTER 54

. . . .

Another myth, to moi is, not getting enough deep sleep, they say, your brain, will automagically, go into that mode, to get more deep sleep, to fix your brain!!!

That again, is bs to moi!!!

Because I saw a, gp on the 14/3/18, she thought my, Mi watch was stressing moi out!!! It saying, I wasn't getting enough, deep sleep, so I took the watch off, in front of her, and put it in my coat pocket, I thought??? My first night, with no more, Mi watch, I thought I'll get a good nights sleep, due to nothing timing moi!!! But nope, still feel like, you know what, I'll say, but hold on, you dirty minded readers!!! Still no luck, and it's been 3 weeks now!!! Still feel like??? But now light sleep then into Deep sleep, but for a short time like 38 mins, I think 8 mins of light sleep, then 38 mins of Deep sleep again, then back to light sleep for, 20 mins I think??? Then Deep sleep again, still short tho, I really don't know why???

How I stumbled across, getting more deep sleep, it's too sleep nude!!! Another 50/50 for you???

CHAPTER 55

. . . .

I thought??? Yeah, yeah??? As a gambling fool, I thought, why not???

And low and behold…

It worked!!! I had 3 hours and 3 minutes, how do I know, I hear you ask moi???

It's my Mi watch, but tied to an ex-phone strap, so not worn on my wrist anymore!!!

That's the thing, about sleeping nude!!!

It lets you body breath well and your skin!!! Like no more watch chocking you skin!!!

Well not tied, because it's a watch, but with an open clasp, so not a string, just clasped it, to a neck string, which I wear now to sleep now!!! As it can still pick up my heart rate and that's how, I know!!! My best result was, 4 hours and 1 minute of deep sleep, but kinda strange now???

It seems like, my broken body has adapted to sleeping nude, like I just get 2 hours something???

Feel kinda 50/50 on most days, bad but still able to function well, just my noggin doesn't hurt like it use to, with under 3 hours of deep sleep.

CHAPTER 56

....

The rat race??? My take on that situation is, trading your time for money, or I'll put it down as my thinking??? Trading your time, for the devils children!!! Aka imps, which is money the devils children, I just DON'T FEEL LIKE DOING THAT, AS I'm STILL HERE!!!

CHAPTER 57

....

I think???

We all, have a fairy watching over us, or taking down notes, on the things we do in this life, because I think???

That book is your life story, it will decide on, where you spend eternity???

I think???

My fairy is called, Isabella??? I don't know why??? I've got a Spaniard, watching over moi???

CHAPTER 58

I've thought of away, to keep the national bus services, in every country, too keep on trucking, when we run out of diesel!!!

It's too use, well filtered out used vegetable oil with vodka added too the mix, or my go go juice, then you know it's all natural, to make the fuel, substance more volatile, and the bonus is…

It's 100%, O natural!!! With the smell of fish and chip, coming out of the exhaust!!! If chippie veg oil used???

CHAPTER 59

I think???

I've found away, too replace the unleaded and diesel we use now??? Just NO MORE POLLUTION???

My thinking is an all natural fuel, I know all of yee is thinking/saying, **HOW**???

Well my thinking goes???

Alcohol and water, or **JUST ALCOHOL**!!! As water can, destroy an engine!!!

My thinking goes, alcohol is similar to petrol, because on the news, a man drank fuel, because it acts like alcohol, and it catches fire easily like petrol, make alcohol the normal way, add boiled water to make more of the liquid, **WHY BOILED WATER???**

BECAUSE THE LIME SCALE, HAS BEEN REMOVED FROM THE WATER, IF YOU LIVE IN THE SOUTH OF ENGLAND???

But that is also another 50 50, because water can destroy an engine!!!

And alcohol has a bit of water in it, as it was formally a living plant needing water to live!!!

How can you remove the water found in it???

Well I have 2 ways, it can be done???

1st way is a little dangerous, put the alcohol in a container and boil it, too 103c, so the water turns into steam, then you'll be left with 100% alcohol.

My 2nd way is only dangerous, if your a fool too play with, liquid nitrogen it'll be used to freeze the water found in the fuel, my thinking or memory goes back in time, to when Terminator 2 the film just came out, it was on, BBC show called "Blue peter" where the host poured, a bit of alcohol into a glass tub, and dipped it into liquid nitrogen, the water in the alcohol froze the glass tube, and 100% pure alcohol was left in the tube.

If lets just say, 10% of alcohol was added to boiled water, will that still ran the engine??? That'll be good!!!

I've thought of another way, too save the engine if rich???

Now can golden engine sleeves/titanium sleeves be made too slipped into the engine???

As both of them materials can with stand water well sort of, or can another Maclean F1 engine be made???

As gold is a natural metal, I believe it'll be able to with stand the water, produce by that fuel.

Water found in engines, I didn't know that'll be a poor combination!!! As it'll eat the engine away from the inside!!!

If 100% alcohol fuel was made??? I'll give it a name of, **GO GO JUICE!!!** But new info I had is alcohol is, 10% down on power, compared too petrol, and this is where titanium engines come into play, as titanium is 45% lighter then steal, so I think??? Lesser power produced, the lighter material, makes it even???

And takes my broken mind back, too hearing on the news, someone drank petrol, because it acts like alcohol!

So have I come back, too replace fuel both types used now??? O yeah and there are YouTube videos, showing what I've suggested!!! So more then 50 50 again!!! It'll be 100% natural then, but you just need time to do it/so???

I've also thought of who can do the job???

It'll be, the government of that country, producing both types of fuel!!! So I'm making the government a fuel supplier, to get you to work, to fund the government back to them!!! So your country will keep on running!!! If the veg oil made??? I think??? It's a 100% alcohol into 100% veg oil so they can sell the fuel all year round!!!

I've thought of another way, so you can get a discount, on the fuel.

It'll be anybody???

Who works in the food industry, it's only 3p off, if 50p per litre of go go juice, then 47p a litre, if bio diesel used 33p, so 30p per litre.

I didn't realise, that alcohol boils, at a lower temperature!!! 78.37 C, may need something to collect the alcohol steam, like boiled water, that'll be 100 % alcohol!!! If left in an open container, it maybe all gone, well properly 8 % less???

CHAPTER 60

••

It's just pure irony!!!

Because now!!!

I've found out how to make, bio diesel and I owned a 306 turbo diesel, and the kick in the nut is!!!

My dad use to own, a Chinese restaurant, meaning free fuel or used cooking oil, if I had the time to do the work??? I'll say, HELL YES MEE NIGGAR, FREE FUEL!!!

But can I/could I, live with the oxygen pipe popping out, every now and again???

That's why I changed to a Honda Civic 1.8 vti, because it had VTEC!!!

Well I would of used coffee filters to clean out the oil, my thinking goes, place netting in first, then grab a funnel, on top of the netting, then coffee filter paper on top of the funnel, and netting over the funnel, so a triple oil filter, the netting takes the big chunks of food out, from the oil, then passes through to the coffee filter, so it'll grab any small bits of food, in the oil, then on to the last bit of netting or another coffee filter used??? It'll catch any thing the last filter missed???

I know there'll be, some cheek people out there??? Who get 333 litres of fuel, and quit there job!!!

So that they'll get the discount, and store the fuel somewhere??? And use it slowly, but if done???

The government, will tax you again, for the same amount of fuel taken??? For 3 years!!!

PS/Nb.

This is just, my view on this situation??? No not the sports wear!!! New balance, it's Nota bene, meaning, Note well.

I just don't know, how or why, I just DON'T TAKE, the lime light or spot light, I just let them have it or there claim to fame, even tho, I could out shine them, but I still DON'T!!!

It kinda feels like, I've been given a challenge, to either, milk my brain injury, or just let things slide??? Because he knows, I use to be, an easy going FOOL and not be bother by much, do I??? Still keep that attitude, after having my brain knocked about??? Or do I become, a ME, ME FOOL???

Being smart, it can only be, narrowed down to, a certain subject/categorise.

Are you smart enough, to speak 12 languages, fluently???

And being smart, you kinda stop learning!!! New things, because you think??? You're way to smart, to learn new shit!!! But there is, no finishing line, to being smart, it's always a wip!!!

And another YouTube video, hey I'm just a, curious cat meow.

It was on about, x's on your palm, if 1 so so life, 2 is another, 50 50 at you, they say, you'll be remembered, for a long time!!!

That is another, 50 50, will it happen too moi??? As I'm bring the cure to Dementia, too England.

Or will this book, be released???
If reading this, thank you!!!

PPS.
Nah, I had a think???
I'll have to draw this out, so it's kinda, worth your money!!!

This has just come to mee broken mind!!!
I've been sent back, to become a COLLECTOR of???

If you thought??? I'll leave 3 pages blank!!!

AH, you can read my, busted mind!!! As I, kinda dropped off hints on the way, that I will!!!

Come back on track, busted ass dead fool.

I'm a collector of???

Of stamps!!! Nah I, just can't give the game away!!! I'll let your mind WONDER???

Did you just turn, a load of pages???

To find out what??? I've become??? It'll be a qui or yes!!!

Because I'm driving you now!!! And I'm just smile at you!!! Due to your curiousness.

As you all think???

Life's all about the, moo cohos denero, aka money!!!

Well, it's not!!! As a Chinese saying goes, "a person goes, to heaven!!! The money, stays in the bank!!!" Because money, isn't accepted in heaven!!! Because it's a physical object, and you enter into, the sprit realm, when your body gives up on you???

I know you think life, life is an easy ride, with lots of money!!! That's why you're after lots of it.

But life's, all about, causing trouble!!!

Because god, has done his own movie, of your life down here!!! Following logic!!!

If you step out into, the unknown???

God will be watching a new movie, of your life on Earth!!! That's why, I'm telling you this!!! Or typing it out, pour tu (for you!!!).

Another 50/50, life choice for you too choose???

I thought of another reason, why I'm still alive now, as God, done another version of sending moi back to Earth, it's due to, moi developing ocd, as I now work for a charity shop now!!! As I'm steaming washed, 2nd hand clothes, I steam them, to looking like new clothes, I also put pride into my work done!!! It's partly down to moi, putting a physiological spin, on your mind!!! New looking clothes, but 2nd hand tho!!! Do I reach into my pocket, and shell out some mooches (money) for it???

PPS2.

This came to, my broken mind, about circumcision, it's the devil!!! He has been, around the world, with his touch!

I can do, an example for tu(you), take your hands, put glove on them, it'll reduce the feeling, same like a foreskin, take the glove off, more touch/feeling, same as with a foreskin, but extra sensitive!!!

Due to it being down below!!!

If they had the snip??? They lose, all that good feeling/ fine touch, I believe, that's why, some men are less sensitive, due to losing there fine touch, or loss in there manhood, down below!!!

O no!!!

Another YouTube video, about charging smartphones, but I think it was, edited, to fit it or to suit the title of the video???

I mean the logical thinking, behind it works well, but I've kinda changed it. But not time it, due to it being my bed time, well the quicker way, or my way or the high way, o no, that was, or is the lyrics to Limp bizkit song "My way", it's to tear a bit of tin foil, the same shape or length, of your phone, and I used a wireless charger as well, so I tucked my phone in to sleep, or to be charged, so I just lay, the tin foil on top of my phone, with a bit of tissue paper used, so the tin foil doesn't rest on the phone, so there is a thin gap between the tin foil and phone, so it'll be like tucking your phone too sleep, my thinking goes, if wireless charger used??? I did place a strip of tin foil, on top of the charging matt, then put my phone on top!!! And nothing happened!!! That's how I know, the tin foil send charge back to the phone!!!

Part of the energy goes up, into the air and the foil returns it to the phone??? In the video, he wrapped the phone up with copper wire/cable, and wrapped the coil cable in tin foil.

Then he plugged the phone in to be charged, I think??? Then edit video, to make it look like it worked, or suited the title of the video???

It was charge a phone, in 20 seconds.

Another 50 50, for you too try, will it work for you??? Well not that quick, I think??? It offers a placebo effect more like 30 mins, or more depending on how empty your phone is???

And another thing is, I've done it, have a piece of card board, wrapped in tin foil, ½ the size of the phone, placed in to the phone case, it seems to make the phone last longer, I've not timed it, but has a placebo effect, in making the phone last longer, another 50 50 thing, for you too, try out???

PPS 3.

Had another think about???

When random D, came out to play, it was summer of 1996, as we/I moved into, Green Lane, Ford, I just felt, board of living, nothing to do!!! That's when I decided, to life gamble, 11 years, before my accident!!! And I also heard on the radio, at the age of 14, you decide on your path in life???

So my brain injury, has become my excuse for me now!!!

But I still don't blame it, that's just moi, take me/leave me, to be???

And another thing is, I've died, and God sent moi back, to be a random fool, because no 1, else is down here, is being random!!! Will you be random, as well now, after reading this???

As of the summer of 2018, the UK, was kinda hot!!!

I know people, during sweating, want a shower right there and then!!!

Please can you, not do so!!!

Because sweating, is slowly cooling you off!!! If having a cold shower??? You've giving your body, a cold shock to the system, which will lead, you to being ill, see quick gain, long term pain!!!

It's another 50/50 at you, well I kinda remember doing that ages ago!!! But didn't have the science knowledge to help moi, understand why???

I think???

I maybe back too, replace petrol and diesel??? As there are, YouTube videos showing, or calling there diesel cars, high mileage hero!

As God, can hear all of us, down here!!!

I just can't believe, he heard moi!!! My thinking dates back too, 1998 or 2003 sometime??? I can't quite remember if, it was before, I could drive or not??? That's why them two dates???

Had another think???

It was when I still was in, secondary school, but had knowledge back in the 80's, as I didn't like alcohol at a young age!!! And knew it catches fire easily, why not use it as the fuel replacement???

Ooo kinda of thought of, another way, too distinguish fuel pump used, petrol/diesel!!!

All is needed to do is, have a smaller extended nozzle, like a straw length and size, too fit in the netting hole on the fuel tank entrance, so you'll only poke a diesel fuel pump into the tank!!!

So have a, net on top of diesel cars it, so only the correct fuel or pump is used!!!

Like you pick up the normal petrol pump still the same nozzle, but diesel pump has a small nozzle on the end!!! The only difference is…

Fuel tank, will you take it too, an open hole like on all cars we have now. Or will it be a net covering the fuel tank hole???

So only diesel pump small enough, too fit in the hole!!!

I know there will be…

A crazy person spraying fuel every just to fill up, there car!!!

Because they think???

Fuel needs to go in CAR!!!

For it to run, moi home, too bed!!!

So any fuel sprayed, close to the open fuel is good enough pour moi!!!

Now too all the car manufactures???

I know I'm a cheeky fool, if my idea used, on all your new cars now??? Can I just ask for, a 12.5% return, on all the cars, with my idea, and I'm only ask for, 12 years income from sales!!!

Then you can keep the rest, as you have a work force to pay, or pay for you too develop newer models, or just do a small donation to brain injury group UK every year???

Or you can have a laugh with, just 3p out of the millions you made???

Or feel whatever your comfortable with???

As this life is…

The choices you, make init brov or sis???

Now you've read the book!!!

AHHH.

I think???

You have too try, a coffeetea.

If available in a whole country.

Why not try it???

Just think???

I'll bite the bullet, on the head!!!

And give it ago.

- Hey you, only live once, so get it done!!! please???
- You'll probably try this??? A mocha chino instead, mocha add, a cappucchino???
- Hey why not, push the boat out??? A tea bag as well, mocha tea chino??? (I think??? Mine and your body, can only do 3 flavours max??? Anymore??? It's just flavoured water!!!

<u>End???</u>

Printed in the United States
By Bookmasters